Splendours of
Islam

Splen

Wilfrid Blunt

اسلا

ours of

am

Angus and Robertson (UK) Ltd
& Robert Harding Associates

Published in Great Britain in 1976 by
Angus and Robertson (UK) Ltd
2 Fisher Street
London WC1

in association with

Robert Harding Associates
5 Botts Mews
Chepstow Road
London W2

House editor: Ellen Crampton
Design: Jonathan Gill-Skelton

Printed in Italy by New Interlitho, Milan

ISBN 207 95682 0

Contents

Colour Plates

To May

Foreword

I have been set an almost impossible task: to compress into a mere thirty thousand words a comprehensive survey of the architecture and arts of the whole world of Islam – from Morocco to Delhi and Samarkand, from the seventh century to the twentieth. It is easier for a camel to go through the eye of a needle. . . .

This book is aimed at the general reader: at, let us say, those who spell Koran with a 'K' and who scarcely recognize the holy book of Islam when it is written 'Qu'rân'; at those who think of the Prophet as 'Mahomet', considering this as acceptable by long usage as are 'Virgil', 'Avicenna' or 'Naples'.

Where 'Mahomet' is concerned, I have the support of Fowler's *Modern English Usage* in rejecting the recommendation of scholars:

The worst of letting the learned gentry bully us out of our traditional . . . *Mahomet* (who ever heard of *Mohammed*[1]

& *the mountain*?) is this: no sooner have we tried to be good & learnt to say, or at least to write, *Mohammed* than they are fired with zeal to get us a step or two further on the path of truth, which at present seems likely to end in *Muhammad* with a dot under the 'h'. . . . Ordinary mortals should go on saying, & writing in newspapers & novels & poems & such general reader's matter, what their fathers said before them.

This book, I repeat, *is* for the general reader.

But we are not yet out of the wood. 'Samarkand' rather than 'Samarqand', surely? But 'Kazvin' or 'Qazvin', the 'Kutb Minar' or the 'Qutb Minar'? For one who knows no Arabic, such decisions are doubly difficult to make; but I am inclined to agree with T. E. Lawrence that the matter is really of no great importance.

Unlike Ibn Battuta (1304–77) I cannot claim to have travelled through the whole length and breadth of Islam; I have therefore gratefully to acknowledge the help I have received from Sir Olaf Caroe, Mr John Semple, Mrs Mildred Archer and other friends who have come to my aid over the architecture of places I have never had the good fortune to visit. Several passages from *A Survey of Persian Art*, edited by Arthur Upham Pope and Phyllis Ackerman are quoted by kind permission of the Oxford University Press. I must also thank Mrs Ellen Crampton for her watchful editing of my text and her invaluable assistance in collecting and selecting appropriate illustrations. Once again Miss Charmian Young was my efficient typist.

No attempt has been made to provide more than a brief list of books for further reading. However, a number of these contain bibliographies which will guide the reader who wishes to go more deeply into some particular aspect of Islamic art.

Finally – for sins of commission I beg forgiveness; for sins of omission I plead lack of space.

W.J.W.B.

[1]The 'Mahomet' of this famous story was not in fact the Prophet, but a Turkish fakir who rashly predicted that he would make a nearby mountain come to him.

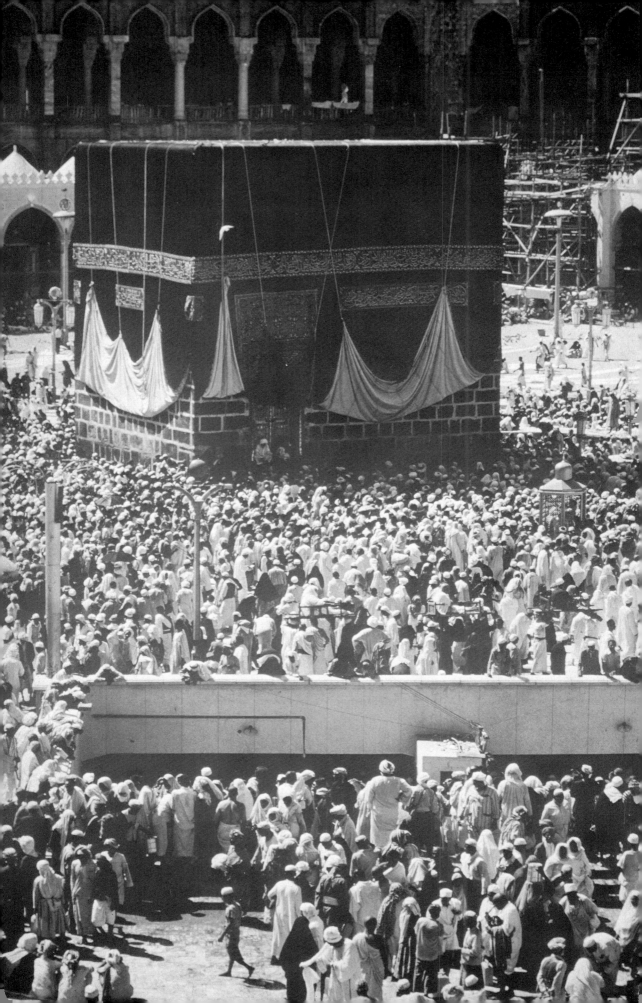

Mahomet

OPPOSITE

The ka'ba, Mecca.

Fourteen hundred years ago there was born, at pagan Mecca in the stony deserts of Arabia, a boy destined to be the founder of one of the enduring religions of the world – Islam.

Whereas the founder of that other great monotheistic creed, Christianity, died before he was forty, Mahomet was already past that age when, after long meditation, he first emerged from relative obscurity to proclaim the existence of the One God to whom all owed complete submission (*islam*). Growing bolder, this Meccan tradesman and one-time caravan leader soon declared himself the last chosen prophet of God, successor to Abraham and Jesus Christ, divinely called to complete the revelation of God's will. But the Meccans, who derived great profit from pilgrims visiting the *ka'ba* (literally 'cube', the cubical receptacle of the revered black meteorite) and miscellaneous local idols, rose in their wrath, and in 622 the prophet without honour in his own country was obliged to flee to Yathrib (Medina), where he met with a friendly reception. With him went his cousin and loyal supporter Abu Bakr, whose daughter he had recently married. From the year of this Hegira (*hijra* – 'flight' or 'separation') the Muslims still date their (lunar) calendar.[1]

The conflict that ensued between Medina and Mecca was finally resolved by a compromise: the Meccans agreed to accept Islam, with Mahomet as the prophet of the One True God, while Mahomet for his part, though insisting upon the destruction of the general run of their idols, was prepared to sanction continuance of the lucrative pilgrimage to the ka'ba. Established soon as master of Mecca, and having despatched envoys to rulers all over the world, Mahomet devoted what little time remained to him to the subjugation of most of Arabia.

This book deals with the art of Islam; we are therefore under no obligation to discuss whether Mahomet was, as Muslims believe, the last great Prophet, the true successor of Abraham and Jesus, or, in the words of H. G. Wells, a man whose 'life on the whole was by modern standards unedifying'. Beyond all dispute, however, was the miraculous swiftness of the dissemination of Islam by means of the *jihad* (holy war). Marching westwards, her armies conquered Spain and invaded France; eastwards they crossed the Indus and reached the frontiers of China: within a century of the death of the Prophet they had become rulers of half the civilized world.

[1] All dates in this book are A.D., not A.H.

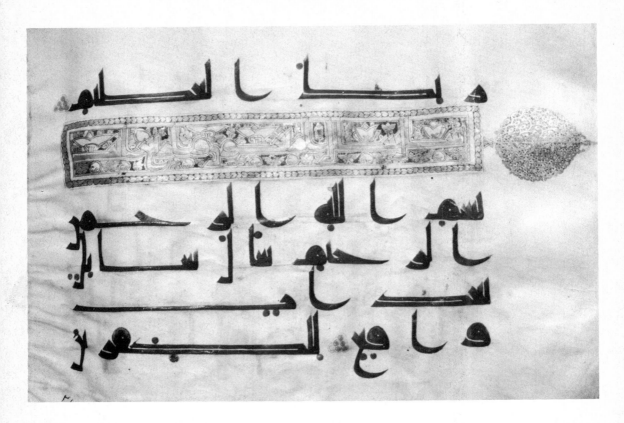

OVERLEAF

ABOVE

Detail from the Koran of Ali, Mahomet's son-in-law.

OPPOSITE

Kufic script in a Koran copied by Uthman Ibn Husayn Warraq, 1073–74

OVERLEAF

The ibn Tulun Mosque, Cairo, ninth century. An early example of the use of the pointed arch, not found in European architecture until three centuries later.

And wherever they went they assimilated and enriched indigenous cultures. H. G. Wells, in *A Short History of the World*, comments:

> In Persia this fresh excited Arabic mind came into contact not only with Manichaean, Zoroastrian and Christian doctrines, but with the scientific Greek literature, preserved not only in Greek but in Syrian translations. It found Greek learning in Egypt also. Everywhere, and particularly in Spain, it discovered an active Jewish tradition of speculation and discussion. In Central Asia it met Buddhism and the material achievements of Chinese civilization. It learned the manufacture of paper – which made printed books possible – from the Chinese. And finally it came into touch with Indian mathematics and philosophy.

From this amalgam of cultures was to arise an architecture of a splendour never surpassed, miniature painting of unparalleled subtlety, magnificent rugs and pottery and tilework, 'arabesques' of fantastic intricacy, and a calligraphic script whose beauty has no rival outside China.

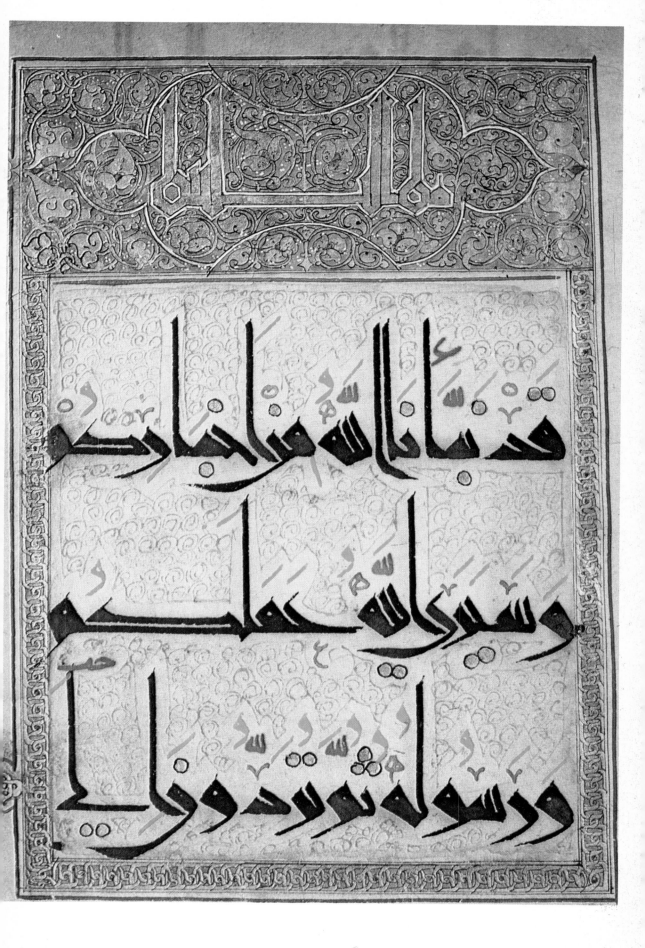

The Early Conquests of Islam | 2

On Mahomet's death, Abu Bakr was elected first Caliph (*khalifa*, 'successor') by the community of Medina. In his two short years of office he completed the conquest of Arabia and despatched his great general, Khalid – known as the 'Sword of Allah' – to attack the Greeks and the Persians; but it was under his successor, Omar, Caliph from 634 to 644 and the first to bear the title 'Commander of the Faithful', that the initial spectacular conquests of Islam were achieved. Omar himself – a giant of a man – remained for the most part at home, directing the campaigns of Khalid and his other generals.

Islam was a faith, and a sword, that moved mountains. In 635, after campaigning in Mesopotamia, Khalid turned to capture Damascus, and a year later drove the dropsical Greek Emperor out of Syria. Victory succeeded victory, till by 644, when Omar met his death by the dagger of a Christian artisan, the Arabs had become masters also of Palestine, Mesopotamia, Egypt and Persia. Under Omar's successor, Othman (644 to 656) – a member of the foremost family of Mecca, the Umayyads – Azerbaijan and most of Armenia surrendered; but Othman, as weak as he was pious, is chiefly remembered as the compiler of the authoritative text of the Koran, the revelations divinely transmitted to Mahomet which constitute the religious and legal code of Islam. The sources on which he is said to have relied were 'scraps of parchment and leather, tablets of stone, ribs of palm branches, camels' shoulder-blades and ribs, pieces of board, and the hearts of men'. The earliest surviving codices of the Koran probably date back to the first century of the Hegira. Othman, too, was murdered – at the age of eighty.

It may be taken for granted that in any religion there will sooner or later – and probably sooner – be schisms and rival factions. In Islam, one faction, the Shi'ites, regarded Mahomet's son-in-law Ali, the husband of Fatima, and their descendants as the only legitimate Caliphs; the other, the Sunnites, believed in an elected Caliphate. Ali was in fact chosen, after much dispute, to succeed Othman as fourth (or by Shi'ite reckoning first) Caliph; but with his assassination in 661 there emerged a hereditary dynasty, the Umayyads, members of the Prophet's own tribe, who because of feuds and doctrinal differences transferred the capital to Damascus and ruled from there with great tolerance for nearly ninety years. It was under

The Umayyad
Mosque, Damascus.
The court of the
Mosque, showing the
little eighth-century
Treasury.

[1]The al-Aqsa Mosque,
also built by Abd al-
Malik, survives but has
been rebuilt several
times.

Abd al-Malik,[1] fifth of the fourteen Umayyad Caliphs, that there
rose in Jerusalem the first great monument of Islamic architecture,
the Qubbat-as-Sakhrah or Dome of the Rock.

Jerusalem and Damascus | 3

Christian, Muslim or Jew; agnostic or even atheist – none can tread the vast area in Jerusalem known as the Haram ash-Sharif ('chief sanctuary'), without a feeling of awe. Here David erected an altar (2 Samuel xxiv, 25), here Solomon built his temple and palace. Two more Jewish temples followed (that of Herod being destroyed in A.D. 70), then came Hadrian's Temple of Jupiter, and finally, in 691, the Dome of the Rock.

For Muslims, the Dome of the Rock is sacred as the spot where Mahomet, miraculously transported thither by the angel Gabriel, ascended by a ladder of light to the seventh heaven to commune with Allah; preserved in it are some hair of the beard of the Prophet, who declared that one prayer there was better than a thousand uttered elsewhere. The Umayyads being no longer welcome in Mecca, Abd al-Malik's original intention had been that the Dome of the Rock should replace the ka'ba as the centre of Islamic pilgrimage.

In reality a shrine rather than a mosque, the Qubbat-as-Sakhrah has been much modified over the years; but the main structural features of the original design have survived. Basically it is a 'Western' building – octagonal and domed, with ambulatories that surround *as-Sakhrah*, the Sacred Rock, which is in fact the tip of Mount Moriah. But Abd al-Malik would hardly recognize its exterior today, for the present dome, dating from 1002 and gilded much later,[1] and the splendid mosaics added to the façades in 1561 by Suleiman the Magnificent, have transformed monochrome surfaces into a glitter of blue and gold. Within, the building displays that exciting fusion of influence so characteristic of Muslim architecture, antique columns and classical ornament rubbing shoulders with the arabesques and abstractions of Islam; but the overall impression given, and one which is emphasised by the magnificent mosaics, is that of a Byzantine building such as the church of San Vitale at Ravenna.

Jerusalem is indeed holy ground; yet how much blood – Christian, Muslim and Jewish – has been spilt for religion's sake in the Holy City! We are told that, after its capture by Godefroy de Bouillon during the First Crusade, the victors, having slain most of the Muslim and Jewish inhabitants, entered the Holy Sepulchre and 'sobbing for excess of joy . . . put their blood-stained hands together in prayer'. One of their first tasks was the conversion of the Dome of the Rock into a 'Templum Domini' –

OVERLEAF

The Dome of the Rock, Jerusalem, A.D. **691.**

[1] The dome is now covered with large crude gilded metal sheets. Photographs in Glück and Diez' *Die Kunst des Islam* (Berlin, 1925) show how much beauty has thus been lost.

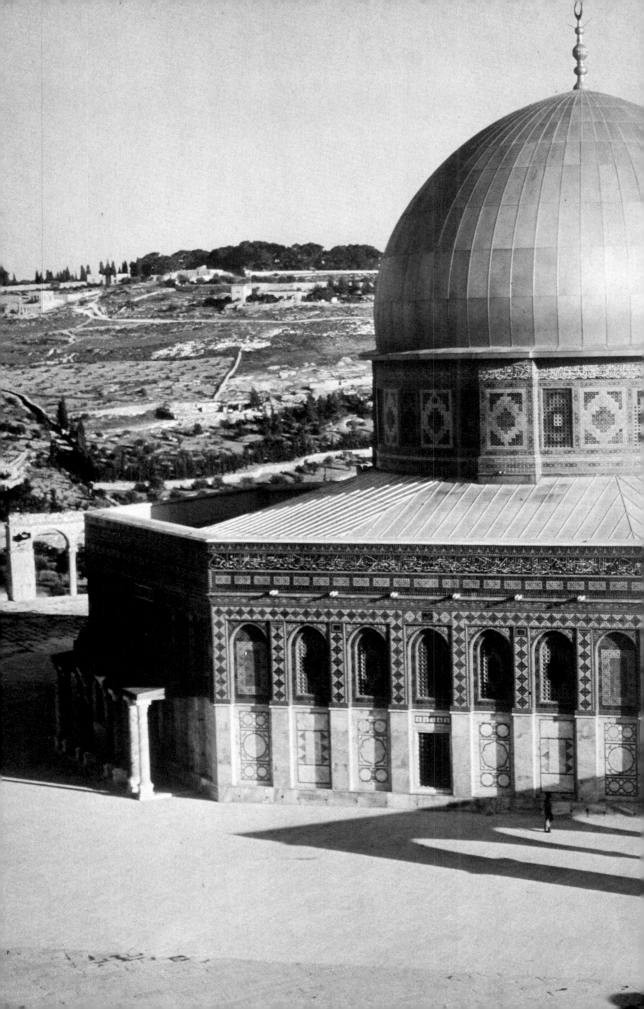

The al-Aqsa Mosque,
Jerusalem, detail of
the minbar. The
Mosque, built in the
seventh century and
rebuilt several times
since, was largely
destroyed by arson
in 1969.

a temple to the glory of the God of Love. After changing blood-stained hands more than once, Jerusalem was finally lost to the Christians in 1244.

The green oasis of Damascus (climb the slopes of Salehiyeh to appreciate its vastness) owes its prosperity, indeed its very existence, to the Barada, the 'River of Gold' and the biblical Pharpar – certainly, as Naiman maintained, a more impressive stream than all the 'waters of Israel'. 'As a man falls flat, face forward on the brook, that he may drink, and drink again,' wrote Kinglake in his *Eothen*, 'so Damascus, thirsting for ever, lies down with her lips to the stream, and clings to its rushing waters.'

It was contact with the late Classical civilization of Damascus that transformed the desert Arab into the cultured town-dweller, and the most splendid surviving monument of the Umayyad age there is the Great Mosque, built by Walid I between 705 and 715. As at Jerusalem, the site chosen was an ancient one, that of a former temple of Jupiter and a Christian basilica which, for a time, existed amicably side by side with a mosque entered by a common doorway. Above one of the walled-up doors of the mosque may still be read a Greek inscription, 'Thy Kingdom, O Christ, is an everlasting kingdom; and Thy Dominion is from Generation to Generation.'

In this building we have for the first time what was ultimately to become the almost universal Islamic design – an 'open court' mosque with a covered prayer hall. 'It is difficult,' wrote Robin Fedden, in his *Syria*, 'to convey a sense of the spaciousness and dignity of the courtyard with its silence and its echoes. . . . The whole place gives a certain agreeable impression of being semi-organic, of having grown and changed and aged in the irregular and unexpected way that people do, rather than of having originated on drawing-boards and in the heads of architects.' Of course it did so grow; and how many of our great Norman cathedrals owe a large part of their charm to additions, subtractions and modifications over the centuries! Arab historians rhapsodize over the richness and magnificence of the Umayyad Mosque in its heyday, and allege in support of its sanctity that no spider dares to weave its web there. Antique columns were collected from all over Syria, and it is said that more than a thousand craftsmen were summoned from Constantinople to embellish the building. The wooden ceiling of the prayer chamber was overlaid with gold, and from it once hung six hundred golden lamps. Of the courtyard, Maqdisi wrote in the tenth century:

> The whole area is paved with white marble. The walls of the mosque, for twice the height of a man, are faced with varie-gated marbles; and, above this, even to the ceiling, are mosaics of various colours and in gold, showing figures of trees and towns and beautiful inscriptions, all most exquisi-

tely and finely worked. And rare are the trees and few the well-known towns that will not be found figured on these walls! The capitals of the colums are covered with gold, and the vaulting above the arcades is everywhere ornamented with mosaic in arabesque designs.

Though some of this glory has departed, the astonishing series of landscape – one ought really to say, townscape – mosaics mentioned by Maqdisi has survived, under pious coats of white-wash applied by fanatical Muslims shocked by their realism; now they may be seen again in all their splendour – one of the most precious legacies of Byzantine craftsmanship. Some of the buildings represented are also found on the walls of churches in Ravenna.

The exquisite little eighth-century Treasury in the court must not be overlooked, and the impressive three-tiered minaret, though largely of a later date, may serve to remind us that it was the Umayyads who, turning for inspiration to the Christian church towers of Syria, introduced this characteristic feature of the Islamic mosque.

Of great interest, especially to archaeologists, are the remains of the 'desert castles' of Syria and Trans-Jordania. They were, in fact, both palaces and centres of economic development, built of apricot-coloured stone by the Umayyads after the manner of the square garrison frontier forts of the Romans, and set in those parts of the 'desert' where a sparse winter rainfall makes the land momentarily 'blossom as the rose'. Much of the ornament of these buildings has been transferred to museums in Damascus, Berlin and elsewhere.

Qasr al-Hayr, an artificial oasis to the north-east of Palmyra, has curious mosaics, murals and plaster carvings, while Khirbat al-Mafjar, to the east of Jericho, is decorated with 'Hellenistic' floor mosaics depicting stags and other animals. At Mshatta, to the south-east of Amman, are the remains of a vast complex built (but never completed) by one of the last and one of the most unorthodox of this line of easy-going Caliphs, Walid II (died 744). Handsome and of enormous physical strength, poet and also musician, Walid led the *dolce vita* at Mshatta, where he filled his swimming pool with wine, used a manuscript of the Koran for target practice, and allowed his mistresses to 'sit in' for him at public prayers when he was not in a mood, or a condition, to appear in person. It seems almost superfluous to add that he was murdered.

The dynasty was played out, the power ripe for the plucking; and in 750 it was duly plucked by the Abbasids – descendants of the Prophet's uncle, Abbas – who were to rule (nominally, at all events) as Caliphs of Baghdad for more than half a millennium.

From Baghdad to Delhi

4

One would not have cared for Baghdad's first Caliph, Abul-Abbas (known as *as-Saffah*, the blood-shedder[1]), and still less for his uncle Abdallah bin Ali, the general who led the armies which overthrew the Umayyads.

Having decisively defeated the last Umayyad Caliph, Merwan II, in battle, Abdallah promised his family generous treatment and invited them to a celebration party at which his ninety too-trusting guests were clubbed to death; he then ordered leathern covers to be thrown over the corpses and had dinner served upon them. Even the bodies of deceased Umayyads were exhumed so that he could have the pleasure of flogging or crucifying their skeletons. Perhaps the only Umayyad who escaped this and subsequent massacres elsewhere – massacres in which Abul-Abbas played an active part – was a certain Abd ar-Rahman, whom we shall meet again later in Spain.

Abul-Abbas was initially established at Kufa,[2] on the Euphrates, but he did not trust the Kufans and proposed to build himself a capital elsewhere; he died, however, before he had found a suitable site, and it was left to his successor Abu Jafar – known as al-Mansur (the Victorious) – to choose the ancient but unimportant market town of Baghdad, supposedly because of its comparative freedom from mosquitoes. Before the century had drawn to its close, the Abbasids – al-Mansur and Harun al-Rashid in particular – had made it the equal of Córdoba (see page 36) as a centre of literature, science and the arts, and vastly its superior in wealth and commerce: and let it be remembered that Córdoba was at that time the greatest city in Europe.

Alas – *ichabod*: the glory has indeed departed! Today not a single Abbasid building survives in Baghdad, and the fabulous city of the Thousand and One Nights has degenerated into what has rather ungenerously been dismissed as no more than 'a collection of evil-smelling mud-brick streets and featureless architecture' in which Rashid Street – 'London's Mile End Road, built of mud and infinitely longer' – is 'the only memento of this caliph of fact, fame and fable'.[3]

Al-Mansur's city was circular, about a mile in diameter, and strongly protected by a series of concentric walls and ditches; thus it was conceived as the well-defended capital of an oriental despot, whereas the Umayyads had treated fortifications, even in their desert castles, more as decorative features than as serious

[1] Oddly enough, the name was really a compliment, designating the liberal host who slaughters his camels for his guests. In Abul-Abbas's case its more obvious meaning was no less appropriate.

[2] Kufic, the earliest form of Arabic script, is said to have originated here.

[3] An anonymous contributor to *Places*, Grosvenor Press, 1954. But may not this street be named after the Rashid Ali of 1941?

25

discouragements to an attacking enemy. In this, as in much else in Abbasid Baghdad, we find (Central Asian) Turkish influences steadily replacing the late Classical and Byzantine of Damascus. In the centre of the city was an immense open space in which stood the Caliph's great palace (the Qubbat-al-Khadrah or 'Green Dome') and the principal mosque. Under Harun al-Rashid, Baghdad grew to a city five miles across within its walls, with – it is alleged – two million inhabitants.

All this splendour, as we have said, has long since vanished – partly as the result of innumerable stormings and sieges, partly because, in the absence of wood and local stone, the Abbasids had often been obliged to use sun-dried bricks and mud. However, of an enormous palace complex covering an area of more than 430 acres, built in the middle of the ninth century at Samarra on the Tigris some eighty miles upstream from Baghdad to serve as a kind of Versailles, enough remains of its two great mosques to give at least a hint of the scale and the style of Abbasid architecture. The gimlet minaret (recalling the Ziggurat of ancient Assyria) of the al-Mutawakkil Mosque (c. 850) – the largest mosque ever built – is of particular interest; but of the palace itself, beyond the foundations, a triple gateway, and some fragments of figurative paintings and almost *art nouveau* stucco wall panels, all has perished.[1] However, the stone walls and some of the vaulting of a late eighth-century desert palace at Ukhaidir, in the remote desert about 120 miles to the south of Baghdad, still stand, and with these as yardsticks it is, I suppose, just possible to accept Professor Grube's conjecture that Samarra was 'probably the most magnificent city the Muslims ever built'. Sassanian architecture was the principal inspiration at both Ukhaidir and Samarra.

By the middle of the ninth century, though the Caliph of Baghdad still ruled in name the whole world of Islam, a number of local dynasties were beginning to establish virtual independence. In Egypt the Tulunids – a dynasty founded by Ahmed ibn Tulun, son of a Turkish slave in the service of the Abbasid Caliph at Samarra who had been sent as governor to Egypt – erected in Cairo in 879 a brick mosque which in general follows Samarran models very closely. Of great interest in this simple but exquisite building is one of the earliest instances of the extensive use of the Saracenic pointed arch,[2] a feature not found in Europe until three centuries later. Those in ibn Tulun's mosque are true 'gothic' (as we in the West rather conceitedly call it), the return of the spring being so slight as to give no suggeston of the horseshoe. It has been claimed that the architect was a Christian prisoner who, saddened by the customary despoliation of ancient monuments, devised a method of building which dispensed with the use of looted marble columns; the style, however, is typically Mesopotamian and the ornament entirely derived from Samarra.

In 969 the Fatimids began their two centuries of rule in

[1] The Germans excavated Samarra, and in Berlin there is a reconstructed wall of the palace, with elegant niches (see Glück and Diez, *op. cit.*, p. 150).

[2] An even earlier pointed arch is to be seen in the second Nilometer on the island of Roda (861), and it was also used to some extent in Syria and elsewhere before Ibn Tulun's time.

Egypt. They were a Shi'ite Persian dynasty of imams who had
consolidated their power in the Maghreb (north-west Africa) and
expanded their empire eastwards. In Egypt they founded a new
city, Al Qahirah (of which Cairo is an Italian corruption), to the
north of ibn Tulun's city. Their magnificent palaces have vanished; but several of their mosques survive, as do three of the sixty
gates – in particular the Bab el-Futuh (Gate of Conquests) and the
Bab en-Nasr (Gate of Victory) – which they built in their city
walls. These superb examples of highly complex military
architecture were designed by Christian refugees, probably
Armenians, from Edessa (Urfa), and show strong north Syrian

influence. It was a Fatimid patron who in 970 founded the oldest still-functioning university in the world – the Al-Azhar.

The Fatimids are, however, perhaps best remembered for their arts – their pottery, rock crystal and glass, woodwork, bronze sculpture, tapestry and embroidery. As John Semple says, by their close connections with Persian ideologies they opened the door to a rich inflow of Iranian aesthetic concepts such as the use of animal motifs. One remarkable specimen of their work is to be found outside Egypt, namely the astonishing painted wooden ceiling of the Cappella Palatina at Palermo (Sicily) carried out in 1142. This 'stalactite' method of roofing a building or a recess was to become a characteristic feature of Muslim architecture; as used in the Alhambra in the fourteenth century it might be considered the Islamic counterpart of the coeval fan vaulting of, say, Gloucester Cathedral.

Eastwards, where the great Muslim general Kutayba had long since carried the banners of Islam to the heart of Asia, we find the Buwayhids, a military family from the south of the Caspian, extending their power over western Iran and much of Iraq. In Nayin, to the east of Isfahan on the fringes of the great Persian desert, they built in the tenth century a remarkable mosque of almost Romanesque simplicity whose intricate stucco work, with grape vine motifs, recalls the borders of William Morris's Kelmscott Chaucer. In 945 Buwayhid princes captured Baghdad and blinded the puppet twenty-second Caliph.

Still further to the east the Samanids established in the ninth century a vast and virtually autonomous empire, centred on Bukhara and including a large part of Transoxiana and Iran. They bequeathed to us one very remarkable monument, the Mausoleum of the Samanids at Bukhara – a cubical domed building of buff-coloured brick which has recently been so thoroughly (yet intelligently) restored by the Russians that it looks almost 'better than new'. A similar but finer building of this kind, with red sandstone 'battered' walls and marble dome, is the fourteenth-century tomb of Tughlak Shah at Tughlakabad, near Delhi. Dating also from before the Mongol cataclysm is Bukhara's so-called 'Tower of Death' – the minaret of the Kalayan Mosque. Built in 1127 of honey-coloured bricks so disposed as to produce a texture like that of an 'Aran' knitted sweater, it rises above a complex of religious buildings to a height of nearly one hundred and fifty feet. From its summit muezzins once called to prayer, watchmen scanned the horizon for the approach of an enemy army, and tyrants hurled trouble-makers to their deaths.

Near the south-eastern corner of the Caspian and close to the present Soviet-Iranian border there rises suddenly, from an artificial mound and overlooking the wide Turkoman plain, an extraordinary and highly abstract monument: the Gunbad i-Kabus. Is this 'great earth-coloured pencil', this gigantic phallus, this super-silo, a watch-tower? No, it was erected in the year

1006 by a local ruler, Shams al Maali Kabus, King of the Ziyarids, to receive in due course his body: which all too soon it did, for six years later he was assassinated. Kabus had ordered that his mortal remains were to be suspended high up in the tower in a crystal coffin, but no trace of this remains: even the Pharaohs failed to find a way of defeating grave-robbers. The tower is now 165 feet tall; but archaeologists have found that a further 35 feet of brickwork exists below ground, and it is therefore probable that it once rose a clear 200 feet above the plain.

It may be on account of its gaunt, functional appearance that the Gunbad i-Kabus is so extravagantly praised today: Robert Byron considered that it ranked 'with the great buildings of the world'. But (to judge from photographs) the twin 'victory towers' at Ghazni, between Kabul and Kandahar, are far more attractive. It was in 997 that Mahmud of Ghazni freed himself from the yoke of the Samanids and by his military skill soon gained control of eastern Persia, much of Afghanistan and a part of northern India. The 'victory tower of Mahmud', the less interesting of the two, has, however, now been shown to date from more than a century after Mahmud's day.

The superbly ornate tower of Mas'ud III, erected in 1114, is, like its sister tower, in cross-section an eight-pointed star; this produces a delightful 'folded screen' effect. Above each once rose a cylindrical superstructure which must have brought the total height of Mas'ud's tower to about 140 feet[1]; they now wear little tin hats which one feels they might almost doff as a greeting. Byron describes the towers as being of 'rich toffee brick tinged with red, and adorned with carved terracotta of the same colour'.

The Ghorids (1163–1206) took over from the Ghaznavids, and to them we owe the minaret at Jam, in remote mountainous country some two hundred miles to the east of Herat. Its beauty and its almost perfect state of preservation fully justify the sensation caused in the world of Islamic scholarship by its chance discovery, as recently as 1957, by an airman off course.

In 1193 a Ghorid prince, Muhammad, captured Delhi, which within six years became the capital of a kingdom that extended over the whole of the northern Indian plain from the Indus to the Brahmaputra. Muhammad himself had returned to Afghanistan, leaving as viceroy his Commander-in-Chief and former favourite Turki slave, Qutb ad-Din Ibak. In 1206 Muhammad was assassinated, and Ibak proclaimed himself Sultan of Delhi, thus establishing the so-called 'Slave' dynasty which continued until 1288.

Near Delhi Ibak erected the earliest Islamic monument in India – the Kuwwat al-Islam Mosque. Adopting what was soon to become the standard practice, he took over a Jain temple and colonnaded court, demolished the temple itself (which stood in the centre of the court), and constructed a Mecca-facing western wall with mihrabs and screens of arches. In addition he began the

[1] The superstructure of Mas'ud's tower survived into the age of photography, and a drawing of it, after a photograph, is given in Upham Pope, *A Survey of Persian Art*, 6 vols, Oxford University Press, 1939, p.984.

building of a minaret, the famous Qutb Minar, which was completed after his death.

The Qutb Minar is an impressive tiered structure, ribbed and of red sandstone, rising to a height of 238 feet. The architect was undoubtedly a Muslim; but the work was carried out by Hindus, who cannot have enjoyed being made to use material taken from twenty-seven 'idolatrous' temples. That great Moorish traveller Ibn Battuta, who in the middle of the fourteenth century explored every corner of the Muslim world, said of the Qutb Minar that it had 'no equal in all Islam. . . . The passage is so wide that elephants could ascend by it.' Complete nonsense, of course! James Fergusson, writing more than five hundred years later, went even further, considering that 'both in design and finish [it] far surpasses any building of its class in the whole world,' and that Giotto's campanile in Florence, 'beautiful though it is, wants that poetry of design and exquisite finish of detail which marks every moulding of the Minar'. Some may feel this praise to be exaggerated. The Qutb Minar was also for a time crowned with a Victorian hat, or cupola.

Just outside the courtyard of the Kuwwat al-Islam Mosque stands one of the most elegant and delicate of early Islamic buildings in India – the tomb of Sultan Altamsh (or Iltutmish), who died in 1235 after saving India from the wrath of Jenghiz Khan. This red sandstone mausoleum (which may once have been domed) is decorated internally with lace-like carving in low relief; it would hardly seem out of place in Fez or Marrakesh.

In 1300, Ala ad-Din, the megalomaniac Khilji ruler of Delhi at that time, began to add to the mosque a further minaret intended to be more than twice the height of the Qutb Minar. Of its projected five hundred feet less than ninety were ever built, and his other mammoth projects fared no better; but he is responsible for a handsome domed gatehouse (1310) to the mosque enclosure.

Though many other splendid buildings were erected in India under the five dynasties[1] that ruled the country between 1206 and the fall of Delhi to the Timurid prince Babur in 1526, our wild scamper through the length and breadth (and thirteen centuries) of Islam will allow us to give only the briefest mention of them when, in Chapter 16, we return to the story of art and architecture in India under the first six great Mughal Emperors.

[1] The Slave-Kings (1206–88), the Khiljis (1288–1321), the House of Tughlak (1321–1412), the Saiyads (1414–50) and the Lodis (1450–1526).

The Invasion of Spain

5

We have followed the eastward advance of Islam; her advance westwards was no less spectacular. In 707 Arab armies reached the Indus, in 708 the Atlantic; how fantastic an achievement!

We may pause a moment on the westward march to note that about 675 a mosque – that of Sidi Okba – had been built in Qairawan (Kairouan), Tunisia, which though subsequently much enlarged and often restored still stands, and which remains one of the holiest in all Islam. However did the Arabs do it? Montgomery did not find time to build a cathedral at El Alamein in 1942!

In 711 a certain Musa was governor of North Africa under Caliph Walid I of Damascus. In that year – on Thursday 30 April, to be precise – Tariq, the Berber general in command of Musa's armies in Mauritania, crossed the Straits of Gibraltar (Jebel-Tariq: 'Hill of Tariq') with a tiny force and advanced through an almost unresisting Spain; indeed, if Joseph Reinaud[1] is to be believed, it was wiser to run than to resist, for Tariq 'killed his prisoners, and served them up as rations to his troops'.

Elsewhere in Europe few tears were shed over the fate of the remote Iberian peninsula; but when, in 718, the Muslims crossed the Pyrenees and advanced northwards through France, all Christendom trembled. Then, fourteen years later, came the decisive battle near Poitiers which drove the invaders for ever from Frankish soil. Before long, northern Spain was lost to them also; but more than seven centuries were to pass before the Catholic sovereigns, Ferdinand and Isabella, completed the reconquest of the south.

And had not the tide of Islam been stemmed at Poitiers, might not all Europe have been overrun? As Gibbon wrote in his famous fifty-second chapter:

> A victorious line of march had been prolonged above a thousand miles from the rock of Gibraltar to the banks of the Loire; the repetition of an equal space would have carried the Saracens to the confines of Poland and the Highlands of Scotland; the Rhine is not more impassable than the Nile or Euphrates, and the Arabian fleet might have sailed without a naval combat into the mouth of the Thames.

'From such calamities,' Gibbon continued, was 'Christendom delivered. . . .' Yet one great benefit would undoubtedly have accrued from a stable Muslim occupation of a substantial part of

[1] *Invasions des Sarrazins* . . ., 1836, quoted by Richard Ford in *A Handbook for Travellers in Spain*. Other authorities speak of Tariq's clemency.

[2] 'Arabic' numerals reached Baghdad from India about 773 and gradually spread from there throughout the Arab world. They were not in use in Christian Europe until the twelfth century.

Europe at that time: the much earlier introduction of Arabic numerals.[2] Probably nothing more delayed the advance of science there than the clumsiness of the Roman. How, say, did one multiply MDCXIII by XCVII?

But to return to southern Spain, where Arabs, Moors and Berbers have bequeathed to us those imperishable monuments of brilliant inventiveness which each year draw thousands of visitors to Córdoba, Seville and Granada.

In the year 785, Abd ar-Rahman I, the Umayyad refugee from Damascus who had established himself as Amir in the one-time Roman city of Córdoba, began the building there of the Great Mosque (Mezquita), which was to be continually enlarged until by 990 it covered an area little less than that of St Peter's in Rome. You enter it across an aromatic courtyard where fountains play in a grove of palms and orange trees and, suddenly within, find yourself in another forest — a forest, or quincunx, of columns. There were once twelve hundred of them, but now no more than eight hundred and fifty: second-hand, monolithic columns of jasper, porphyry, *verde antiche* and other precious marbles, many looted from Nîmes, Narbonne, Seville, Tarragona and Carthage, though a hundred and forty of them were the gift of the Emperor Leo in Constantinople. All are surrounded by double tiers of polychrome arches.

Then, in the very centre of the forest, you stumble upon something as disconcerting and as unexpected as a Jonah in the belly of the whale: a flamboyant Renaissance Christian cathedral. The Emperor Charles V, who did not at that time know Córdoba and so had not appreciated the enormity of the crime when he sanctioned the erection of the building, cried out when later he saw the desecration: 'You have built here what you, or anyone, might have built here or anywhere else; but you have destroyed what was unique in the world. You have pulled down what was complete, and you have begun what you cannot finish.' The reproof would have come better from a man who had not himself disfigured the Alcazar in Seville and torn down portions of the Alhambra to build a palace that remains to this day unfinished.

Most precious of all is the Chapel of the Mihrab, finished in 965, in which brilliant use is made of the trefoil arch. The plaster filigree and the mosaic work, too, are incomparably beautiful. In the little octagonal sanctuary, beneath a roof formed of a single block of marble in the shape of a conch, was once a manuscript of the Koran, bound in gold encrusted with pearls and rubies, several pages of which were traditionally ascribed to the hand of Othman himself. The worn marble paving-stones bear witness to the millions of faithful knees which over the years made the obligatory circumambulation of the sanctuary.

The Mezquita, mutilated though it has been, remains for all to see. But almost totally destroyed is the fabulous palace of Az-Zahra, the Córdoban Versailles built about seven miles from the city by Abd er-Rahman III (891–961) for his favourite wife, Zahra (the Flower). Even when allowance has been made for the exaggerations of Arab historians, it is beyond doubt that in the closing years of the tenth century Córdoba was by far the greatest city and centre of learning in Europe. We read in Reinhart Dozy's *Spanish Islam* of 'its half-million inhabitants, its three thousand mosques, its hundred and thirteen thousand houses, and its twenty-eight suburbs'. At a sober estimate its population was not less than three hundred thousand; Richard Ford speaks of 'nearly a million' inhabitants, while Joseph McCabe in *The Splendour of Moorish Spain*, rejects the 'nearly':

> In the tenth century Cordova had a population of a million souls, a lavish supply of pure water, and miles of well-paved and lamp-lit streets. . . . There was not [at that time] anywhere in Europe, outside Arab Spain and Sicily, and there would not be for at least two centuries, a single city with 30,000 people, with even the most rudimentary sewerage, with any paved or lamp-lit streets, with a communal supply of pure water, with an elementary regard for hygiene, with a single public bath (and few, if any, private baths) or school, and with even moderately good precautions against theft and violence.

Recent excavations of what *The Times* described as 'an Arabic Pompeii' have confirmed the former splendour of Az-Zahra.

Córdoba, Spain. The eastern entrance of the Great Mosque.

But the great days of Córdoba were nearing their end. After the death in 1002 of Mansur, a Córdoban nobleman who had seized the reins of power during the minority of the feeble Caliph Hisham II, a palace revolution led to the fall of the Spanish Umayyad dynasty. However, there is another great flowering of Islamic architecture yet to come in southern Spain, culminating in the Alhambra at Granada, and the legacy of the Muslim occupation can also be seen in Toledo, Seville, and many other towns. Its influence is still far from dead: how much, for example, does not contemporary Spanish music, both classical and popular, owe to it! But how many Córdobans now remember that the river on which their city stands, the Guadalquivir, is none other than the Wad-al-Kebir — the 'Great River' of the Arabs?

The Seljuk Turks

6

In the eleventh century the Seljuk Turks, nomads from the Kirghiz Steppe and converts to Sunni (orthodox) Islam, marched southwards through Turkestan, defeated the Ghaznavids, and then swarmed into Persia. By 1034 they were masters of Khurasan, and twelve years later their chief, Toghril Beg, entered Baghdad. Here the current Caliph, a puppet whose strings were manipulated by the Shi'ite Buwayhids, welcomed the arrival and support of an orthodox Muslim, created him 'King of the East and of the West', and in due course offered him his daughter in marriage. However Toghril died before the nuptials could take place.

Toghril was succeeded by Alp Arslan (1063–72) who, in spite of moustaches so long that they had to be tied down before he could shoot, conquered Asia Minor and took the Greek Emperor prisoner. He was followed by Malik Shah (1072–92). Both were great builders, during whose reigns there was a flowering of splendid, simple, dignified architecture and also much achievement in the field of minor arts, especially ceramics. Two other remarkable men, their Vizir Nizam al-Mulk (the patron of Omar Khayyam) and his deadly rival Taj al-Mulk, Chamberlain to Malik Shah's mother, were powers behind the throne and responsible respectively for the erection of the wonderful great and small dome chambers in the Friday Mosque in Isfahan, Malik Shah's favourite place of residence.

Impatient tourists, attuned only to the glitter of Persian tilework, have been known to 'do' the Friday Mosque without even discovering the existence of these two plain brick dome chambers; some never even get beyond the Safavid sparkle of the buildings that surround the Maidan (main square). The dome chambers are, admittedly, dry wines: an acquired taste. But even the uninitiated, if they pause a little, will soon come to sense something of the serenity of their structure, of the perfect resolution – especially in the smaller chamber – of the problem of setting a circular dome upon a square base. Eric Schroeder well estimates the magnitude of the achievement of these Seljuk architects:

> European dome-builders never approached their skill. How ingeniously the Western builder compensated his ignorance of the mechanics of dome-construction is attested by the ten chains round the base of St Peter's, and the concealed

[1]Upham Pope, *op. cit.*, p. 1008.

Lustre bottle from
Rayy (near Tehran),
twelfth or thirteenth
century.

cone which fastens the haunch of St Paul's. But engineers could not hope to prescribe an ideally light dome of plain masonry before Newton's work on the calculus. The Seljuks, however, had *solved* the difficulties which Wren *avoided*. Not that they knew anything of the calculus: their knowledge was empirical. But by courageous experiment and intelligent observation of failure the Seljuks built in the twelfth [*sic*] century what is practically the ideal dome, made possible by the advance of mathematical science in the eighteenth.

Further Seljuk mosques exist elsewhere in Persia, especially in Ardistan, Kazvin and Gulpayagan, but time has treated these less kindly. They all show what was from now on to be the typical Iranian mosque design, based on pre-Islamic Iranian palace architecture, in which each side of the court is interrupted centrally by an ivan (arch leading to a chamber). The principal prayer chamber, usually domed, contains the *kibla* ('direction' wall) and mihrab (niche) pointing towards Mecca. There are also at Maragha, a small town to the south of Tabriz which is chiefly remembered as the capital of the Mongol Hulagu Khan, three Seljuk tomb towers of great beauty. The most attractive, the Gunbad i-Kabud (Blue Dome), built in 1196, is a terracotta-coloured polygonal brick tower, originally domed, with walls netted like a [cantaloup] melon and relieved with tiles of the purest turquoise imaginable.[1]

In 1077 Asia Minor was converted into a fief for one of the

Samarkand bowl in brown, white, red and yellowish-green, ninth or tenth century.

[1] Robert Byron is mistaken in describing the brick as 'plum-red'.

41

OPPOSITE TOP

The Friday Mosque,
Isfahan, Iran.
Exterior of the
eleventh-century
great dome chamber,
built, of course,
before the days of
glazed tiles.

OPPOSITE BELOW

Mausoleum of the
Samanids, Bukhara.
A cubical, domed
building of buff-
coloured brick,
tenth century.

OVERLEAF

Al-Azhar Mosque
973, Cairo. The
mosque of the
world's oldest still-
functioning
university.

younger Seljuk princes, Suleiman, who established there a dynasty known as the Sultanate of Rum. This endured until 1302, the country being spared the full flood of destruction left in the wake of the Mongol invasions which in 1242 put an end to Seljuk rule in Persia. But during the last fifty years of the Sultanate its rulers were vassals of the Mongols.

Mas'ud I (1116–56) made Konya his capital. Situated on the south-western edge of the vast central plain of Asia Minor, watered by many streams and surrounded by orchards of plum and apricot, this pleasant town was the ancient Iconium where Paul met, circumcised, and adopted as his most cherished disciple his 'dearly beloved son' Timothy. But it was not until a century after Mas'ud's time, when the Mongol wolves were already howling at the door, that the Sultans of Rum erected, at Konya and elsewhere, a number of remarkable buildings of a character quite different from that of Seljuk monuments in Iran. The mosques, madrasas (theological colleges), khans and tomb towers of Asia Minor, being built of stone, have fared far better at the hand of time than have their brick counterparts in Persia. If we exclude the Great Mosque at Damascus, which belongs to a more classical tradition and had little subsequent influence, these Seljuk buildings in Anatolia constitute the first real stone architecture in Islam. The Egyptians turned to them later for inspiration.

It was during the reign of Ala ad-Din Kai Kubad I (1219–36), known as 'the Great', that Rum entered upon its brief period of splendour. Poets, savants, artists and dervishes, fleeing before the ruthless Mongol hordes, sought refuge in Konya and elsewhere in the Sultanate to bask in the munificence of Ala ad-Din. Then in 1236 the Sultan was poisoned by his son and successor, the weak and luxury-loving Khusru II. But the cultural momentum was not immediately arrested, and two of the most interesting surviving buildings in Konya, the Karatay and Ince Minare madrasas, date from 1251 and 1258 respectively.

The Ala ad-Din Mosque, in the citadel of Konya, was built in the time of Mas'ud I but in its present form dates principally from about 1220, when Ala ad-Din summoned an architect from Damascus to refashion and extend it. The prayer hall, with its eleven aisles of grey stone columns, is frankly Syrian in style. Very different in conception are the dome-chamber mosques, without courts, of the Karatay and Ince Minare madrasas.

The Karatay, which is now a museum of ceramics, has a splendid portal of honey-coloured marble and, internally, brilliant turquoise and wine-coloured glazed-brick faience;[1] this was a form of decoration which the Seljuks were the first to make use of on a large scale. The Ince Minare Madrasa was once dominated by an enormously tall needle-like minaret (ince means slender), the upper part of which was destroyed by lightning in 1901;[2] with its huge spreading dome, and its minaret reduced to a

[1] The design is curiously 'spiky', and Derek Hill (*Islamic Architecture and its Decoration*, Faber, 1964) reproduces a photograph of a local thistle which closely resembles it.
[2] But photographs showing it in its entirety exist (see Glück and Diez, *op. cit.*, p. 236).

stumpy chimney, it looks like a cross between a planetarium and a crematorium. Its ornate portal, of light red stone and stucco, is most extraordinary: more curious, perhaps, than beautiful. What, one wonders, inspired these broad straps of Arabic calligraphy, looped above the door, which give it an almost Indian flavour; we find something rather similar at Jam (see page 33). Odder still is the almost baroque portal of the Ulu Cami at Divrig, built in 1228. Murray, in his *Handbook for Travellers in Asia Minor* (1895 edition), surprisingly considers it 'of surpassing beauty', but it appears to lack any kind of unifying rhythm.

In discussing the Abbasid, Samanid and Fatimid dynasties I have made hardly a mention of their 'minor' arts, in particular of their pottery.

The Samanids produced fine ceramic wares in Nishapur and Samarkand, and the Abbasids (who knew what Chinese T'ang potters could achieve) also made the important discovery of lustre and used it to brilliant effect; but it was not until Seljuk times that we find pottery becoming a major creative activity. To get some idea of the astonishing range and beauty achieved at Rayy,[1] Kashan and elsewhere in Iran by Seljuk potters we cannot do better than turn to the fifth volume of Upham Pope's monumental *Survey of Persian Art*, in which will be found three or four hundred representative illustrations of their work, many of them in colour. It was now in the art of the potter, as later in the art of the book, that Islam was to show that to speak of these as 'minor' arts may be convenient but, if used derogatively, is blatantly absurd.

What a wealth is here — of form and design, of colour and of glazing! There are cups, dishes, ewers, tiles, bottles and hand spittoons (euphimistically catalogued as 'globular flower vases'); there are sweetmeat dishes, rosewater sprinklers, and even 'piggy banks' to encourage thrift; there are occasional figures and animals 'in the round', and it is said that Omar Khayyam designed a pottery bird-scarer. As for technique, we find incised, relief and even pierced ware, decorated with 'slip' and both overglaze and under-glaze painting in brilliant and endlessly varied colours. The subjects treated include separate figures and figure scenes with moon-faced, slit-eyed men and maidens, the former often sporting neatly-trimmed imperials, who clearly derive from Central Asian models. There are animals of many kinds, among them camels, elephants, stags, horses, oxen and hares, and some brilliantly calligraphic birds which might almost have been painted by Picasso. There are plant forms too, and arabesques. And then there is calligraphy itself, the wonderfully beautiful Arabic script being put to a thousand different decorative uses. This was indeed a golden age of ceramics, and it is sad that our 'art potters', their eyes resolutely fixed upon the equally lovely but very different pottery of China and Japan, almost completely ignore this rich mine of inspiration.

OPPOSITE TOP

Pottery from Rayy (near Tehran), late twelfth and early thirteenth centuries.

OPPOSITE BELOW

The Mezquita or Great Mosque *c.* 965, Córdoba. Arches in front of the mihrab.

7 The Ayyubids

In 1157 Sultan Sanjar, last of the Great Seljuks, died defending his territories in eastern Persia against a fresh wave of nomad invaders from Central Asia; they were, after all, only doing precisely what his own ancestors had done a century earlier. He had reigned for forty years.

There now followed a period of great confusion, with numerous atabegs (princes, or regents) ruling in virtual independence in various parts of the Seljuk empire, while the Crusaders maintained a bridgehead along the whole of the eastern shore of the Mediterranean. Then in 1171 there emerged a certain Salah ad-Din al Ayyubi, a Kurd, who deposed the last feeble Fatimid in Cairo and proclaimed himself Sultan of Egypt and Syria; we know him better as Saladin. Jerusalem fell to him in 1187, and on his death six years later the large territories he had conquered were divided up among Ayyubid princes. Egypt was held by the dynasty until 1250, when the power passed to the Mamluks (the word means 'owned') – a non-hereditary military oligarchy of purchased Turkish, Mongol and Circassian slaves from whose ranks a succession of adventurers seized the Sultanate. Soon afterwards the Mongols overran what remained elsewhere of the Ayyubid empire.

The stupendous citadel of Aleppo, though begun earlier, is substantially Ayyubid, the creation of one of Saladin's sons. Fedden calls it 'perhaps the finest example of Saracenic military architecture', and considers its conception to be 'as audacious as it is architecturally impressive'. No photograph can give any idea of the overwhelming scale of the building or of the beauty of its fulvous stone.

In 1176 Saladin established Cairo's first madrasa, that of the Imam Shafi'i, the purpose of which was to propagate orthodox Islam after the Fatimid (Shi'ite) interregnum; at the same time the formerly Shi'ite Al-Azhar University became the world centre and intellectual heart of Sunni learning. Imam Shafi'i's madrasa has long since disappeared; but his mausoleum, built in 1211, is still to be seen in the wilderness of graves to the south of the citadel. Ibn Gubeyr, a Spanish Arab who visited Cairo in 1183, desribes the shrine as 'a magnificent oratory of vast size and strongly built,' standing beside a madrasa so large and so complex as to resemble 'a township with its dependencies'. The Ayyubids

erected further madrasas in Baghdad, Damascus and Aleppo, and further mausoleums in Cairo.

Aleppo, Syria. The Saracen Gate of the Citadel, *c.* 1200.

Court and hunting scenes on Seljuk pottery make it plain that a good deal of other painting, on walls as well as in books, must have been made at that time; but all too little of it has survived. Towards the close of the twelfth century, however, we see the emergence of schools of manuscript illustrators in Mesopotamia and Syria, influenced by Central Asian or Hellenistic traditions. The frontispiece of a *Kitab al-Diryak* of 1199 is a fine example of the former, the illustrations to a manuscript of the *Assemblies* of Hariri (1222) of the latter. A yet more splendid manuscript of Hariri's 'best-seller' – a work which describes in rhymed prose the picaresque adventures of an ingenious old rogue named Abu Zayd – was made in Baghdad in 1237 and shows the fusion of eastern and western influences.

8 | The Mongols

Then came Jenghiz Khan and his Mongol warriors – and once again Europe (but this time it was *eastern* Europe) was to tremble at the approach of Asian hordes. A historian of Bukhara, a man fortunate indeed to have escaped with his life when his city was devastated in 1220, wrote of the new scourge which swept across Asia like a plague of locusts:

> *Amanand, u kandand, u sukhtand, u kushtand, u burnand,*
> *u raftand.*
> The came, they uprooted, they burned, they slew, they despoiled, they departed.

In the course of five years (1219–24) the first wave of invasion ravaged Transoxiana, Afghanistan, and northern Persia as far as where Tehran now stands, the Mongols obliterating the cities through which they passed, raping the women and then exterminating every living creature. They say that half a million people were slaughtered in Merv alone, where the famous library was also totally destroyed. While one Mongol army reached the banks of the Indus, another broke through the Caucasus to overrun southern Russia. Jenghiz Khan died in 1227; but his generals, his sons, and in due course his sons' sons carried on his work of conquest and destruction, and four years after his death a fresh invasion gave the Mongols control of all Persia. A further attack on Russia resulted in 1238 in the fall of Moscow, and in 1241 an army of Poles and Teutonic knights was defeated at Liegnitz, Silesia – little more than a hundred miles from Prague and Dresden. Then in 1241 the sudden death of Ogedei, Jenghiz Khan's successor, sent the contenders for the throne scurrying back to Central Asia to stake their claims to the Khanate. The advance was halted: Europe was saved.

As the Bukhariot historian wrote, the Mongols laid waste, killed and continued on their way. But the time came when they settled, absorbed indigenous culture, and began to rebuild. Hulagu, Jenghiz's grandson and brother of the then regnant Great Khan, having seized Baghdad in 1258 and finally overthrown the Caliphate, founded the dynasty of the Ilkhans of Iran, who ruled successively – and at first gloriously – from Maragha, Tabriz and Sultaniya in north-west Persia for eighty years.

'Thank God,' cried Hulagu, 'I am both a world conqueror and a would preserver!' Two of his tomb towers at Maragha survive in

LEFT

'Battle between
Jenghiz Khan and
Jelal ad-Din, 1221.'
From a Persian
manuscript, early
fifteenth century.

OVERLEAF

'The Caliph of
Baghdad prepares to
surrender his
beleagured city to
Hulagu, grandson of
Jenghiz Khan.' From
a Persian manuscript,
early fifteenth
century.

part (the Seljuk buildings have lasted better), and on a hilltop
outside the town are minimal remains of his famous observatory.
The greatest of the Ilkhans were the brothers Ghazan Khan[1] (1295–
1304) and Uljaitu (1304–1316). The former on his accession became
a Muslim, made Islam the state religion, and chose Tabriz for his
capital. With the aid of his brilliant viziers Rashid ad-Din (author
of histories of the Mongols and of the Universe) and his rival Raj
ad-Din Ali Shah, he created, wrote René Grousset, 'probably one
of the most beautiful cities the world has ever seen'. Upham Pope
goes so far as to call him 'one of the greatest builders of Asia,
possibly greater as a builder than Timur [Tamerlane], whose
creations were regional, or than Shah Abbas, whose masterpieces
were largely confined to a single city'. Yet of Ghazan's own
mausoleum at Tabriz and the immense complex of buildings
associated with it, barely a vestige remains, and the two principal
surviving – or in part surviving – monuments of the age were in

[1] It is interesting to recall
that Marco Polo, on his
return from China,
acted as escort to a
seventeen-year-old bride
for Ghazan's father,
Arghun. He reached
Tabriz about 1295 to
find that Arghun had
died; the girl was
therefore married to the
young Ghazan.

fact erected in the days of his successor: the stupendous mosque of Ali Shah at Tabriz, better known as the Arg, and the mausoleum of Uljaitu at Sultaniya.

Acts of God (earthquakes, frequent and severe in that part of Persia) and the no less destructive hand of man have left to us but a tiny fraction of what was achieved architecturally in those marvellous opening decades of the fourteenth century in Iran; it is as though, of the age of Wren and Vanbrugh, we had nothing left beyond documentary evidence, the chit-chat of travellers, the roofless east end of St Paul's (stripped of all its ornament), a badly-bombed Castle Howard, and some fragments of one or two City churches. But let us look at what does remain.

The Arg at Tabriz is colossal, and in its nakedness as austere as a Norman Castle. The great brick vault, now fallen, once spanned a space of one hundred feet (Gerona Cathedral in Spain, the largest brick vault in Europe, spans only seventy-five); the architect clearly set out to surpass (and he did) the Taq i-Kisra at Ctesephon. All that is left of the Arg is a gaunt façade, one hundred and twenty feet high, built of exquisitely laid buff-coloured bricks. 'Today', writes Upham Pope,

> the ruins stand bleak, but we must reclothe them with smooth translucent stone and see them enveloped with the ultramarine blue faience illuminated with gold which was once the omnipresent glory of Tabriz, all reflected in the great pool punctuated by the foaming jets of the fountain; and within, bronze encrusted with gold and silver, handsome window grills, rich polychrome stucco, and gorgeous silver and enamelled glass lamps. It was certainly one of the greatest buildings ever created in Iran, in sheer size approached by few organic structures . . .

Within, as Sir Roger Stevens notes, the most conspicuous feature is now a public lavatory: surely the only loo in the world with a wall thirty-four feet thick!

At Sultaniya – the 'Imperial' city – a tremendous dome rises like a roc's egg from an octangonal egg-cup, the whole dwarfing a sprawling village of mud hovels as does the Roman amphitheatre at El Djem in Tunisia. Lapis lazuli and turquoise tiles still cling here and there to the base of the rosy-buff dome – the largest in Iran – like colour notes on a sepia sketch. The eight minarets are now little more than roughed in. The whole is a husk, a skeleton whose bones the imagination must clothe again with the blue robes of their vanished splendour. How much longer can it hope to survive – for time is certainly running out? Till the next major earthquake? But money is short, and what is available for restoration is spent on the buildings of Isfahan and those other cities that draw the hurried tourist. Only the *aficionado* of Islamic architecture makes the rather laborious expedition to Sultaniya.

There is, of course, Mongol architecture to be seen elsewhere in Iran, but nowhere on so grandiose a scale. In particular, there is exquisite stucco work in the mihrab of Uljaitu (dated 1310) in the Friday Mosque in Isfahan, in the sanctuary of Pir i-Bakran (1299–1312) and at Ashtarjan (both near Isfahan); scholars seem to disagree as to whether the wonderfully ornate stucco work in the Gunbad i-Alaviyan at Hamadan is Seljuk or Mongol. The motifs have sometimes an almost *art nouveau* flavour.

Relatively little Islamic painting survives from the days before the coming of the Mongols and their adoption of the faith in 1295; but from the early part of the fourteenth century onwards some impressive manuscripts were written and illustrated in Tabriz and elsewhere. Various influences – Baghdadi, Seljuk and Chinese – are visible in the work carried out in different centres; it is therefore not possible to select any one book as representative of the age. But a splendid example showing Chinese influence, with emphasis on line rather than colour, is an incomplete copy of Rashid ad-Din's *Universal History*, the earlier surviving part of which (dated 1306, with seventy miniatures) belongs to the Edinburgh University Library, the later (dated 1314, with one hundred miniatures) to the Royal Asiatic Society. Made for the author at Tabriz and under his supervision, it is the most important known manuscript of the Il-Khanid school.

In ceramics, though Rayy had by 1300 been obliterated for ever by the Mongols, splendid work continued to pour from Kashan (equally famous for its scorpions), Sultanabad and Sava; the star-shaped tiles of Kashan are particularly lovely. And if nothing has so far been said of textiles, metalwork and glass, it is only because in this headlong rush through the splendours of Islam there is no time or space to mention more than a fraction of what was achieved.

When in 1335 the Ilkhan Abu Sa'id, who had reigned for eighteen years, died without issue the Mongol kingdom of Persia fell apart, leaving the way open for a new wave of invasion from Central Asia.

9 | The Mamluks of Egypt

With the capture of Baghdad by the Mongols in 1258 and the subsequent murder of the Caliph and most of his family, the Abbasid Caliphate in that city, long impotent, was finally extinguished after more than half a millenium. However, a scion of the family who had managed to escape to Egypt was accepted by the Mamluk Sultan, Baybars, as Caliph, but given no secular power. Cairo now became and remained until the coming of the Ottoman Turks in 1517, the centre of the Muslim world.

This Baybars, who ruled from 1260 to 1277, was 'a blue-eyed Turk from Kipchak afflicted by a cataract which had caused him to fetch but £20 in the slave market' at Damascus. Having achieved power by a combination of military skill and total lack of scruples, he proceeded to drive the Crusaders out of most of Syria, to repulse the Monguls and to extend his authority over a large part of Arabia and Nubia. Under a succession of Turkish and Circassian Mamluks many splendid mosques, mausoleums and private houses arose in Cairo. There is now much Syrian and Mesopotamian influence, the former particularly noticeable in the use of polychrome stonework such as one finds in, say, the exterior of Orvieto Cathedral (1310).

From the time of Sultan Qalaun (1279–90), whose name means 'duck' in Mongol, we have a huge complex containing a maristan (hospital and medical school), a madrasa and his mausoleum. The maristan, which it is said the Sultan was stirred to build by his own recovery from a severe illness, anticipated – and indeed surpassed – our National Health Service: treatment was free, and the patients were entertained by music and uplifted by regular readings from the Koran. Later it became a madhouse. Externally there is a lack of elegance, the minaret, in particular, being a foursquare tower of Western solidity rather than Islamic grace. The interior of the mausoleum has massive granite columns and is richly decorated with carved and painted plaster; there is also a lavish use of inlaid marbles. The inspiration would appear to be the Dome of the Rock.

The largest and most spectacular example of fourteenth-century Cairene architecture is the madrasa-mausoleum of Sultan Hasan, Qalaun's grandson, who ruled from 1347 to 1351 and again from 1354 until his assassination in 1361; it has been described as 'the most precious gem in Cairo's diadem of medieval monuments'.

Cairo, Mosque of
Muhammad Ali.
Built in the Ottoman
style within the
Citadel begun by
Saladin in the
twelfth century.

The building of it – probably Hasan's only good deed – was begun
soon after he had staged his come-back and, like so much else in
Cairo, was constructed of stone looted from various pyramids.
Though it was intended to have four minarets, each 270 feet high,
the first alone stands as originally planned: the second was replaced in the seventeenth century by something smaller; the
third fell immediately, killing three hundred schoolchildren, and
perhaps for this reason the fourth was never built. Pietro Della
Valle, the Roman globe-trotter who was in Cairo in 1616, wrote
ecstatically of the beauty of the dome, which collapsed not long
afterwards. The madrasa-mausoleum stands on shelving rock
below the citadel, and one would like to have seen the brave
'European gymnast' who about 1450 walked on a tightrope from
the top of the minaret to the citadel.

Entrance to the building (which was of course denied to Della
Valle) is through a superb portal, eighty-five feet high. Inside is a
four-ivan court leading to an impressive *liwan* (prayer chamber)

The Mamluks of Egypt

OPPOSITE

Konya, Turkey.
Detail of the façade
of the Ince Minare
Madrasa, 1258.

with a handsome stone *minbar* (pulpit). Beyond this comes the domed mausoleum containing the simple sarcophagus of the Sultan. The numerous stains on the floor of the tomb chamber, alleged to be the blood of slain Mamluks, may well be bats' urine.

The so-called 'Tombs of the Caliphs' – a misnomer since they are in fact those of later Mamluk sultans – lie to the east of Cairo over the brow of the Windmill Hills; there is a further and less interesting Mamluk cemetery to the south of the citadel. The great congeries of mausoleums in the Eastern Cemetery (a better name for the former) include some of the loveliest Cairene Muslim buildings, the most impressive being those of Sultan Barquq (reigned 1382–99), and Qait Bay (reigned 1468–96). Sultan Barquq's mausoleum and *khanqah* (a sufi retreat for meditation), with two fawn-coloured, herring-bone-patterned domes and two slender minarets (one of them now truncated), were begun by himself but completed after his death by his son and successor, Sultan Farag.

Qait Bay, one of the last independent Mamluk sultans of Egypt, was a forceful character who rose from humble beginnings as a twenty-five-guinea slave, and who is said to have kept himself physically fit when in office by 'flogging the president of the council of state or other high officials with his own arm, with the object of extorting money for the treasury'. The mausoleum and madrasa of this great patron of the arts are notable for a lovely dome netted with arabesques, and an exceptionally elaborate and elegant minaret, one hundred and thirty-five feet tall, with projecting galleries resting on stalactites. Skilful use was made, both externally and internally, of stone of different colours.

Such are one or two of the many magnificent Mamluk buildings in and around Cairo – buildings too often passed over in haste by visitors who think of Egypt merely as 'the land of the Pharaohs'.

In the minor arts, Cairo played an important part in the development of metalwork, the technique of which had been transmitted to them from the Seljuks by way of the Ayyubids. Most collections of Islamic artefacts contain examples of Mamluk ewers, candlesticks and incense burners, many of which are inlaid with precious metals. Calligraphy flourished, and in particular the Korans of the Mamluks are magnificent. To pottery they contributed little of interest, Cairo being at that time flooded with Sung and Ming porcelain; but the enamelled glass, especially the mosque lamps made in Syria in the fourteenth century, are deservedly famous. When Tamerlane took Aleppo in 1403, he was so impressed by what he saw that he carried off the entire glass-workers' guild to Samarkand with the intention of having a monopoly; but unfortunately the craftsmen did not survive the shock of their forced transplantation.

Morocco and Spain

OPPOSITE

Fez, Morocco. The El Karouin Mosque, begun in the tenth century and subsequently enlarged. The Fountain Pavilion recalls the Court of the Lions in the Alhambra, Granada.

From Egypt to Morocco: we make, in a leap from one page to the next, that great journey 'long as the entrails of Omar' that the Arab armies made laboriously nearly thirteen hundred years ago. Go West to go East: there is nothing eastwards, before we reach the borders of Afghanistan, that is so typically 'oriental' as Fez and Marrakesh. For the interior of Morocco, until the country's seizure by the French shortly before the First World War, remained an almost inviolate outpost of Islam. One might reasonably expect to run into Harun al-Rashid in modern Fez, never in modern Baghdad.

Of what the Idrisi (788–1061), the founders of Fez, built in Morocco, little remains. There followed two Berber dynasties – the Almoravids (1061–1149) and the Almohads (1149–1269) – desert nomads from south of the Atlas. The former overthrew the petty rulers who had followed upon the downfall of the Spanish Umayyads, to govern Morocco, Portugal and two-thirds of Spain from their newly-built capital, Marrakesh. It is to the Almohads – Morocco's greatest dynasty, under whom the empire was for a time extended as far as the borders of Egypt – that we owe the tower of the Kutubiya Mosque in Marrakesh and the Giralda in Seville. In 1231 the Almohads were driven out of Europe, and their successors in Spain, the Nasrids (1232–1492), the builders of the Alhambra, brought the world of the Arabian Nights to our very door. In Morocco under the Merinids (1213–1524) Fez was extended and embellished, and from the Sa'adian dynasty we have a late but splendid flowering of Islamic architecture in Marrakesh.

The same architect, it can hardly be doubted, built in the closing years of the twelfth century the triplet mosque towers of the Kutubiya in Marrakesh, of Hassan at Rabat, and the Giralda – now the tower of Seville Cathedral. Hassan's tower was never finished; the Giralda, originally two hundred and fifty feet high, was topped in 1568 by a further hundred Christian feet of rich filigree work so that bells might ring where once the muezzin chanted; alone the Kutubiya, built by Christian slave labour, stands in perfection – a four-square tower of rosy stone with a band of turquoise tiles, rising to more than two hundred feet, and crowned by the famous 'golden balls' which aroused the cupidity of every conqueror of the city. The slender minarets of Asia are exceptional in western Islam.

In 1213 the Berber hordes of the Beni Marin poured across the Atlas 'like the rain, or the stars, or the locusts, for number'[1], overthrew the Almohads, and in due course made Fez their capital. With its famous El Karouin University, Fez had long been the Oxbridge of western Islam, and during the first half of the fourteenth century the Merinids built a little handful of theological colleges which are still the delight of all who visit this magical city. They also added to the enormous and ancient El Karouin Mosque (said to be able to hold twenty-two thousand worshippers) a Court of Ablutions; in this were later erected two fountain pavilions like those in the Court of the Lions in the Alhambra at Granada.

Before Morocco fell to the French in 1911, mosques and madrasas had, of course, been firmly closed to unbelievers. But in the spring of 1914, after the Protectorate had agreed to undertake the care of the country's historical monuments, Fez's appeal for funds to restore their treasures was naturally met by a demand to inspect them. That same summer an Englishman named John Horne, availing himself of the goodwill engendered by French generosity and braving the hostility of the more fanatical Muslims, took a number of valuable photographs which show the mosque and madrasas in all their picturesque decay; these he subsequently published in a book entitled *Many Days in Morocco*. The condition of the buildings at that time certainly distracted attention from the marvellous craftsmanship of the elaborately carved stucco and woodwork; yet something was inevitably lost when the very necessary restoration was carried out, and Horne's photographs therefore constitute an important historical record.

The most attractive of the madrasas are the El Attarin, the Es Sahrij and the El Mesbahiya, all erected about 1321, and the Bou Inania which dates from the middle years of the century. Of these, the last-named is the finest. It was built by Sultan Abu Inan to atone for some very unfilial behaviour which had won for him his father's throne. The cost of the building was enormous; but Abu Inan was so delighted with it that he refused even to check the architect's bill; 'What is beautiful,' he said, 'what gives pleasure to all, is never too expensive.'

Entering the Bou Inania through splendid bronze doors, one ascends a short flight of onyx steps with tiled treads to reach a large courtyard paved with onyx and white and rose-coloured marble. But for the flutter of white doves, a cloistered silence prevails. The walls, above a tiled dado, are of lace-like plaster, broken at intervals by the windows of the rooms of the students. There is – as always – a central pool, and some magnificent pierced cedarwood doors. A tiny streamlet, tributary of the River Fez, separates the madrasa from its mosque, which contains a fine but much damaged minbar. This is also the only madrasa

[1] The *Raod el Kartas* – a history of Morocco written in Fez in 1326.

mosque in Fez which has its own minaret, but in other respects it may be taken as representative.

Approximately coeval with the Merinid madrasas in Fez is that marvel of Islamic architecture, the Alhambra. And when one remembers what it has suffered over the years from (Christian) vandalism, neglect, and ill-judged restoration, not to mention the occasional earthquake, the miracle is seen to be yet greater.

Muhammad I, first of the Nasrid rulers, was of Arab descent, so that even in this last phase of Islamic building in Spain it is not really correct (though it may be convenient) to speak of 'Moorish' architecture. Muhammad made Granada his capital, but it was principally under two later rulers of the dynasty, Yusuf I (1333–53) and Muhammad V (1353–91), that the fortress-palace of Al-hamra – 'the Red' – was built.

Its setting – on a little plateau above the River Darro, approached by steep woodland paths where nightingales sing and water is never silent – is marvellously beautiful. Passing through the Gate of Judgment one encounters first that greatest piece of

ABOVE

Rabat, Morocco. Summit of the Hassan minaret, late twelfth century.

OVERLEAF LEFT

Marrakesh, Morocco. Minaret of the Kutubiya Mosque, late twelfth century.

OVERLEAF RIGHT

Fez, Morocco. Minaret of the Bou Inania Mosque, late fourteenth century.

vandalism, the palace of Charles V. To build it he destroyed most of the Moorish Winter Palace; to pay for it, funds were extorted from the Moriscos (Christianised Muslims) to buy off the dreaded Inquisition, which, nevertheless, was let loose on them. And he did not even finish it. What Wren did at Hampton Court may be forgiven – because he was Wren; Pedro Muchaca was a pedestrian architect, and for him there is no such excuse.

Of the 'Moorish' palace, what can be said that has not been said a hundred times already? Even those who have never visited the Alhambra must be familiar from photographs with the Court of Myrtles, the Court of the Lions (begun in 1377 and formerly the harem), and the Hall of the Ambassadors. As Richard Ford, who in the early 1830s lived for a time within the palace, wrote: 'Lightness was the aim of Moorish architects, as massiveness was of the ancient Egyptians. The real supports were concealed, and purposely kept unexpressed, so that the apparent supports, thin pillars, and gossamer perforated fabric, seemed fairy work; the object was to contradict the idea of weight, and let the masses appear to hang in the air floating like summer clouds.' This ambition is perhaps most spectacularly realized in the roof of the Chamber of the Two Sisters, a 'fantastic honeycomb of hanging stalactites' which seems the work of bees rather than of man. The plain exterior of the building gives little hint of all this opulence within.

Some purists may feel about the Alhambra as they do about the Taj Mahal – its only rival in the Islamic popularity stakes – or the Royal Mosque at Isfahan built by Shah Abbas around the year 1600, that there is something overripe, something decadent, about its rich and ornate decoration, its riot of red and blue and gold tilework and painted stucco. Certainly the Alhambra makes no claim to the austere beauty of the Seljuk tomb chambers of the Friday Mosque in Isfahan; but to the romantic it remains one of the most exciting and evocative buildings in the world. In short:

> Quien no ha visto Granada
> No ha visto a nada

> Who has not seen Granada
> Has not seen anything.

However, the Alcazar in Seville, built in the style of the Alhambra by Morisco architects in the reign of Pedro the Cruel (1334–69) and his successor, is not without its admirers.

Then in 1492, the very year that Columbus sailed from Spain to the New World, the Catholic monarchs Ferdinand and Isabella of Aragon finally succeeded in capturing Granada and driving the Muslims for ever from their last stronghold in western Europe. So for our final example of Islamic architecture in the West we must return to Morocco, to the mausoleum in Marrakesh of the Sultans of the Sa'adian dynasty (1524–1659) with its incredibly ornate stuccowork, delicate as filigree. The Tuscan marble

OPPOSITE

The Alhambra, Granada, Spain. Arches around courts were a classic feature of Islamic architecture.

Hispano-Moresque
dish in lustre, *c.* 1470.

columns which support the roof were paid for, weight for weight, in sugar, which was cultivated in the oasis. Not until 1917, and then only thanks to the popularity of Maréchal Lyautey, was this holy place made accessible to infidels.

Though various crafts, including calligraphy, textile-weaving and the making of knotted rugs, were carried on in Muslim Spain, the most important minor art practised there was that of pottery. It seems to have been principally at Malaga that the *azulejos* (tiles) so extensively used in the Alhambra were made, as also the splendid Hispano-Moresque lustre ware of which the most important (though not the most attractive) pieces are the huge 'Alhambra vases' with winged handles and tapering bases. After the fall of the Kingdom of Granada, Valencia, which had been lost to the Muslims in 1238, carried on the tradition of lustre ware with the help of Moriscos and of Spaniards trained by them.

The House of Tamerlane

11

History – we are told, and have already seen – has a way of repeating itself. In the second half of the fourteenth century yet another tide of destruction swept westwards from Central Asia and engulfed most of the lands over which Jenghiz Khan and his successors had ruled. This new conqueror – this 'monster that hath drunk a sea of blood, and yet gapes still for more to quench his thirst'[1] – was Timur-i-Leng (Timur the Lame), known to the West as Tamerlane.

A Turko-Mongol prince claiming descent from Jenghiz Khan, Tamerlane was born in the year 1336 at Kesh (Shahr i-Sabz – the Green City), about fifty miles to the south of Samarkand. By 1369 he had possessed himself of Turkestan, and after being proclaimed sovereign at Balkh made Samarkand his capital. During the next thirty years he extended his empire by ruthless aggression, seizing most of Persia, advancing through Russia as far as Moscow, and conquering Delhi where he had himself proclaimed Emperor of Hindustan. In 1400 he drove into Syria to defeat the Mamluks at Aleppo and Damascus, and the following year destroyed Baghdad, making (it is said) a hundred and twenty towers of the skulls of its inhabitants. He died in 1405 – on his way to conquer China.

Tamerlane and his successors (the 'Timurids'), like Jenghiz Khan and his, were great destroyers who became great builders. It may not be extraordinary (though it is undoubtedly regrettable) that semi-barbarous nomads from the wastes of Central Asia should begin by flattening the cities through which they passed; it is surely extraordinary that they should systematically spare the lives of craftsmen during these wholesale massacres and so, by acting as catalysts to the very cultures they had apparently sought to extinguish, give rise to new and exciting art forms. The destroyer-turned-creator remains one of those mysteries for which there appears to be no simple explanation. Under the Timurids, tile decoration on large surfaces was to reach its highest perfection.

After the disintegration of the Mongol empire, almost the only reasonably stable government in territories they had formerly held was that established by the Muzaffarids (1314–93) in southern Iran. Here letters and the arts were encouraged by the enlightened Shah Shuja (1357–84), who was the patron of one of Persia's

[1] Marlowe, *Tamburlane the Great.*

69

Herat, Afghanistan.
The last standing and
the recently fallen
minarets of the
Musalla of Gauhar
Shad, *c.* 1432.

finest lyric poets, Hafiz. At Kerman, on the fringe of the great
Persian desert, the Muzaffarids built a magnificent Friday
Mosque which, but for an inscription bearing the date 1349, might
easily be mistaken for Timurid work of sixty or seventy years
later. The same applies to the Friday Mosque at Yazd, which also
probably dates from the fourteenth century. These buildings,
which escaped Tamerlane's wrath, must surely have provided
the inspiration for much that was characteristic of Timurid
architecture.

This is, perhaps, the place to remind the reader of something
important which is easily overlooked by visitors to Iran, Afghanistan and Russian Central Asia. When portions of the stonework of
a western cathedral perish and have to be replaced, the new stone
remains for many years conspicuously out of harmony with the
old. But tiles acquire no patina, and can therefore be replaced
without the repair being visible. In this connection it is very
instructive to examine the photographs of Persian mosques taken
in the 1930s for Upham Pope's great *Survey*. They show, for
example, that the façade of the Friday Mosque at Yazd had lost
almost all of its tilework, and that what one now sees here is
therefore not restoration but brilliant guesswork. The same

Herat. Detail of the brickwork on the minaret of the Madrasa of Gauhar Shad, *c.* 1433.

applies, but mostly to a lesser extent, to the Friday Mosque at Kerman and to hundreds of other Islamic tiled buildings.

Tamerlane had made Samarkand his capital in 1369, but it was not until later in his reign that he could spare time from his endless campaigns to attend to the embellishment of it. Much of what he built has perished; much of what we see today was the work of subsequent Timurids.

We are fortunate in having a lively factual account of Samarkand from the pen of the Castilian ambassador Ruy Gonzales de Clavijo, who was present at the great celebrations held there in 1404, and also two splendidly colourful if less reliable descriptions by native historians. Gonzales de Clavijo passed through Kesh on his way to Samarkand and describes in some detail the magnificent but still unfinished Akserai Palace, of which nothing remains today beyond two mammoth lumps of masonry covered with exquisite tilework in which turquoise and ultramarine predominate.

In Samarkand itself, the buildings most closely associated with Tamerlane are the Gur-i-Mir mausoleum and the mosque and madrasa of Bibi Khanum. The former, which he built to receive the body of his favourite grandson, Muhammad Sultan, holds also his own and those of various Timurid princes. The immense cantaloup-shaped, blue-tiled dome, visible from miles away, stands upon a buff-coloured drum encircled by a white kufic inscription. Noble even in decay are the splendid ruins of the Bibi Khanum. This Chinese princess, Tamerlane's favourite wife, had in fact nothing whatever to do with the great complex of buildings that bears her name; the mosque was simply a Friday mosque ordered by Tamerlane to replace an older one. Work on it started on 11 May 1399 at a moment proclaimed favourable by the royal astrologers, and craftsmen from all over the Timurid world, assisted by 'ninety-five mountainous elephants', were responsible for its erection. A striking feature is the height of the entrance portal, which is loftier than that of Peterborough Cathedral.

On the fringes of the town is the Shah-Zinda, a chain of lovely little mausoleums clinging to a flowery, now tomb-strewn hillside. For the most part they date from the late fourteenth or early fifteenth centuries, and consist of a porch leading to a small tomb chamber; the tilework throughout is exquisite. First to be buried here, and so to sanctify the site, was a certain Qasim ibn Abbas, known as the Shah-Zinda or 'Living King' – a cousin of the Prophet who is alleged to have come to Samarkand in the early days of the Hegira to convert its fire-worshipping inhabitants to Islam, but only to be executed for his pains. The other mausoleums contain the bodies of various Timurid princes and friends of the royal family who either died too soon, or were not considered important enough, to find a last resting-place in the Gur-i-Mir itself.

To pass today from the Shah-Zinda to the Registan is as if to exchange the calm of a country churchyard for the racket of a Piccadilly Circus. The Registan – the hub of Samarkand, on an island site round which trolley-buses ply – was considered by Lord Curzon to be, even in its ruin, the noblest public square in the world. 'I know of nothing in the East approaching it in massive simplicity and grandeur,' he wrote, 'and nothing in Europe, save perhaps on a humbler scale the Piazza di San Marco in Venice, which can even aspire to enter the competition. No European spectacle indeed can adequately be compared with it, in our ability to point to an open space in any Western city that is commanded on three of its four sides by Gothic cathedrals of the finest order.'

None of the three madrasas which give onto the Registan was

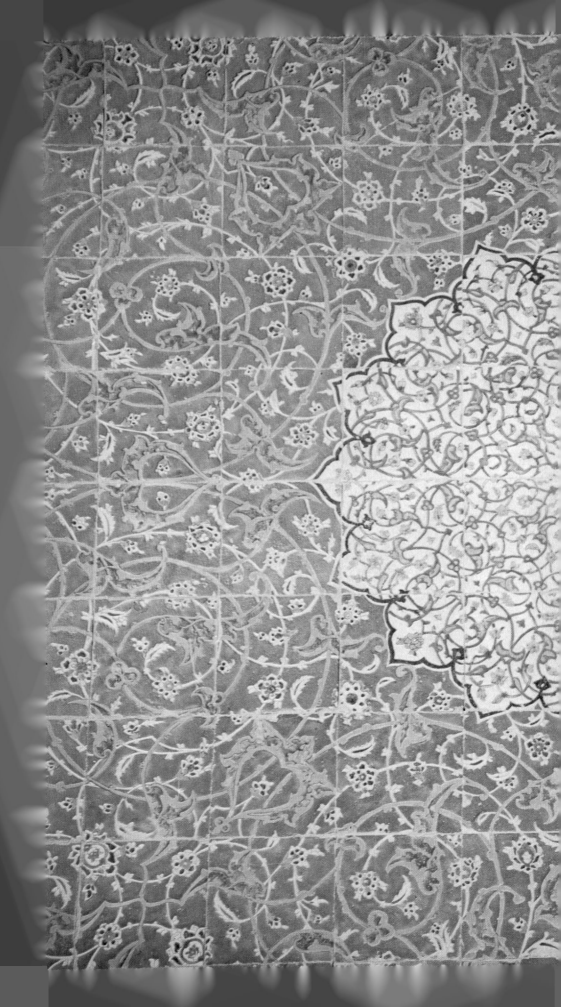

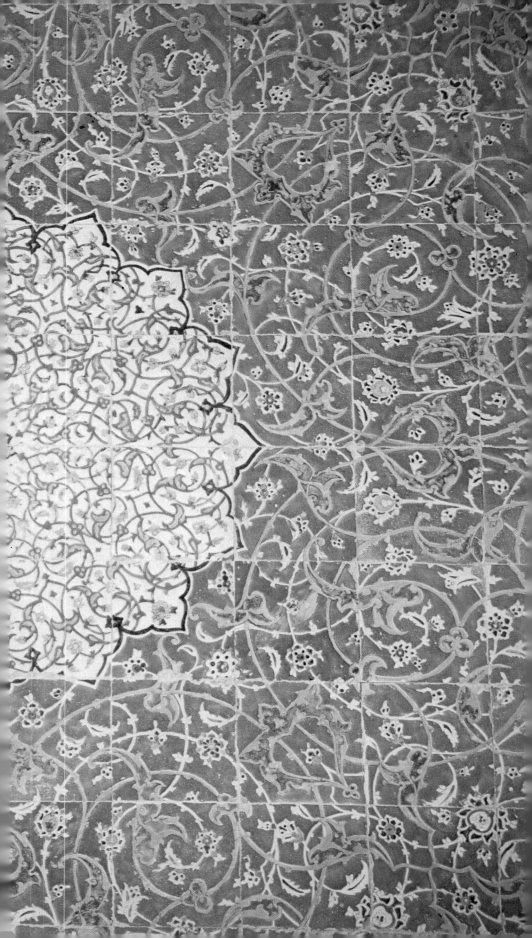

built in Tamerlane's lifetime, though one or more of them may have replaced earlier buildings. The oldest of the existing colleges is that of Ulugh Beg, Tamerlane's astronomer grandson, who is said to have lectured there and who also built an observatory outside the town. Opposite, and clearly in imitation of it, stands the Shir Dar or 'Lion-bearing' madrasa, built in the early seventeenth century and so-named from the crude representations of the Lion and Sun of Persia above the great central ivan; though inferior to its model, it has fared better at the hands of time, and its two turquoise fluted domes still stand. On the north side of the square rises the Tila Kari (or 'Gilded') madrasa, built about the middle of the seventeenth century. Certainly the ensemble is enormously impressive but for many people the Maidan in Isfahan (see page 99), which Curzon only allows to be 'one of the most imposing piazzas in the world' is even finer.

Moreover, Isfahan has kept the encroaching West fairly successfully in check, whereas Samarkand has lost much of the magic associated with its mellifluous name. A hundred years ago the Russian town knew its place; now it has burst its banks and overwhelmed the picturesque, unpractical, insalubrious capital of Tamerlane. Yet we must be grateful to the present Russian rulers for arresting, so far as funds permit, the decay of these lovely buildings that Tsarist Russia neglected. Bukhara, on the other hand, still retains its character; but for how long can it hope to postpone the onslaught of 'progress'? However, it is in Herat and in Meshed, two other chosen cities of the Timurids, that one can best step back into the past.

Four years of unedifying family squabbles followed upon the death of Tamerlane; but in 1409 his youngest son, Shah Rukh, seized Transoxiana and made Herat his capital.

Shah Rukh might have felt at home in the Rome or Florence of the day: he was, in short, a typical Renaissance figure who attracted artists and men of letters to his court and gave them employment, yet a man who could also be as violent and unscrupulous as any Borgia. Even more remarkable was his wife, Gauhar Shad, daughter of a Chagatai Turkish noble, who rose to a position of power and authority rarely achieved in the Muslim world by a woman. She is principally remembered as the creator, together with her architect Qavam ad-Din of Shiraz, of her mosque at Meshed (1405–18), and of a group of buildings at Herat – her mosque, college and mausoleum – known collectively as the musalla (1417–37).

Meshed already had a long history behind it (including an inevitable sacking by the Mongols) when Gauhar Shad began the erection of what many consider the most beautiful extant building in all Islam. The city owed its foundation to the burial there of Harun al-Rashid, who died at nearby Tus while on his way to suppress an insurrection in Transoxiana; it owes its sanctity to

OPPOSITE

Meshed, Iran. The shrine of Imam Reza.

PREVIOUS PAGES

The Friday Mosque, Isfahan. South-west ivan and portal to sanctuary, fourteenth to sixteenth centuries.

the bones of Reza, the eighth Imam, who also died at Tus; but its architectural glory it owes to the beneficence of Gauhar Shad and the genius of Qavam ad-Din. Non-Muslims will regret the sanctity of the golden-domed shrine of Imam Reza, which unfortunately extends to the whole complex, for the Unbeliever must generally rest content with a God's-eye view of Gauhar Shad's court from the museum roof or the top of a minaret.

Robert Byron's description of the court has often been quoted, but cannot be bettered:

> The whole quadrangle was a garden of turquoise, pink, and dark blue, with touches of purple, green and yellow, planted among paths of plain buff brick. Huge white arabesques whirled above the ivan arches. The ivans themselves hid other gardens, shadier, fritillary-coloured. The great minarets beside the sanctuary, rising from bases encircled with Kufic the size of a boy, were bedizened with a network of jewelled lozenges. The swollen sea-green dome adorned with yellow tendrils appeared between them.
>
> But in all this variety, the principle of union, the life-spark of the whole blazing apparition, was kindled by two great texts: the one, a frieze of white *suls* writing powdered over a field of gentian blue along the skyline of the entire quadrangle; the other, a border of the same alphabet in daisy white and yellow on a sapphire field, interlaced with turquoise Kufic along its inner edge, and enclosing, in the form of a three-sided oblong, the arch of the main ivan between the minarets . . .

The latter inscription tells us that Gauhar Shad built the mosque at her own expense, and that 'Baysunghur,[1] son of Shah Rukh, son of Timur Gurhani [Tamerlane] wrote this inscription, with hope in God, in the year 821 [A.D. 1418].'

Even more spectacular in its day, but now little more than a memory, is Gauhar Shad's musalla at Herat. It consists — or consisted — of three distinct buildings: the musalla proper (mosque, or place of prayer); her madrasa, in one corner of which is her fluted, blue-domed mausoleum; and the mausoleum of Sultan Hosain Baiqara who ruled Herat in the closing years of the fifteenth century. Until a hundred years ago all these were in part standing, though in various stages of decay. It was then that, under the threat of a Russian advance from the north, all buildings likely to provide cover for the enemy were demolished by Afghan labourers on the advice, if not under the direct orders, of the British. So perished, but for its minarets, the musalla — by general consent the finest complex of buildings in the Muslim world.

Of the four minarets of the musalla, two were destroyed by an earthquake in 1932, and a third fell in the early 1950s; there now remains (but for how long?) a single yardstick by which the glory of the whole building can be measured. It emerges from a polygonal base as intricately ornamented as the finest carpet. The circular

[1] Shah Rukh and Gauhar Shad's youngest son. Ulugh Beg, the eldest, acted as viceroy for his father in Samarkand.

drum is decorated with bands of white lettering and lozenge-shaped patterns; it culminates in the honeycombing that once supported the balcony, and finally a diapered net of white faience. The overall colour of the decoration is a softly glittering pale blue, relieved by a deeper blue, pure yellow, Indian red, a gentle green, and white; it is a hundred and fifty feet high, and only a photograph taken from a helicopter could hope to give any idea of its beauty. Gauhar Shad's minarets at Meshed seem, by comparison, no more than rough sketches for the masterpiece at Herat, and no doubt the rest of the mosque was also proportionately more miraculous. Of the madrasa of Gauhar Shad, a double-balconied minaret and the mausoleum are still fairly intact. Four minarets, tottering and mutilated, shedding their tiles like autumn leaves, mark the corners of the madrasa of Hosain Baiqara.

About two miles to the north-east of Herat, charmingly situated on the first foothills of the Paropamisus, is Gazur Gah, the shrine of a certain Khwaja Abdulla Ansari who was stoned to death by schoolboys in the year 1088. But the shrine in its present form was the work of Shak Rukh, who erected it at the time his wife was building her musalla, and the place has now become a necropolis. The tilework is varied and remarkable; there was close contact with China in Timurid times, and some of it appears to show Chinese influence.

It is a great misfortune for the hurried traveller in the Middle

ABOVE

Shir Dar ('Lion-bearing') Madrasa, Samarkand, 1619–36.

OVERLEAF

Herat. Detail of the brickwork on the dome of the Mausoleum of Gauhar Shad, *c.* 1432.

OPPOSITE

**The Friday Mosque,
Isfahan. Decorative
work on the mihrab
of Uljaitu, 1310.**

East that most of the best Timurid buildings are off the beaten
track. There is, for example, the shrine of Nasr Parsa at Balkh,
splendid even in decay but very inaccessible. There is Turbat
i-Shaikh Jam, in so squalid a village on the Afghan-Iranian
border that those who have ever spent a night there prefer to
forget it. Tabriz, near the Turkish frontier and now at last linked
to Tehran by the railway, has besides the Arg the battered remains
of the once noble Blue Mosque, built in the 1460s but only after
the Timurids had been driven out of north-west Persia by
Turkoman tribesmen. Its tilework is dazzlingly beautiful, but the
setting utterly sordid and unromantic. Apparently some kind of
restoration – long overdue – is at last in hand, and perhaps this
will include the banishment from its precincts of a school play-
ground and quantities of wire netting.

In Isfahan, Timurid work can be seen in parts of the Friday
Mosque, especially in a fine faience recess near the mihrab of
Uljaitu and in the south-west ivan. There is also a small mausoleum, the Darb i-Imam – not far from the Friday Mosque but rather
difficult to find – which has what is probably the best Timurid
tilework in the city.

The most important Timurid contribution to architecture was
the development of faience to adorn the surfaces of their buildings.
The existing palette of self-coloured tiles was enriched until to
turquoise, black, white and lapiz lazuli had been added various
shades of yellow, emerald green and an aubergine which
fluctuated through garnet to a tone that was almost black. The
Timurid builders inherited the tradition of tilework merely as an
ornament quite subsidiary to structure; they left behind them
buildings that glowed and glittered with colour, but whose
structural qualities were not swamped or obscured by it. As
Robert Byron wrote:

> At a first glance the chief characteristic of the new style is
> ostentation. Domes and minarets protrude and multiply;
> portals, *ivans*, and niche-façades attain extraordinary height;
> patterns and texts become exuberant in proportion to their
> intricacy . . . unbridled, fantastic; colour achieves a range, a
> depth, and a brilliance not equalled before or since . . .
> Aesthetically, the achievement of the new style was to devise
> a method of displaying colour without prejudice to an appear-
> ance of stability and coherence. This it did by the propriety
> of its general proportions and detailed ratios, by splitting the
> ornament into fields related to those elements, and by a subtle
> display of reveals, bevels, and kindred means of emphasis
> and punctuation – by using, in fact, a language common to all
> good architecture. Timurid buildings sit the ground, and
> prove that their architects, though providing a show in two
> dimensions, were still able to think in three.

12 The Timurids and the Art of the Book

As in architecture, so in the art of the book the Timurids set a standard never surpassed in purity, and by their successors the Safavids in sumptuousness only.

Tamerlane himself was too occupied, first with his wars and then with his building, to play any notable part here, though is known that he had book-binders brought from Egypt and Syria. Samarkand, however, made little contribution to the art that was to flourish so vigorously under Tamerlane's successors. It was his son Shah Rukh who, by attracting to his court a host of painters, craftsmen and calligraphers, of scholars, scientists and musicians, was to make his capital, Herat, the Asiatic equivalent of the Florence of the day. Shiraz was probably the cradle of Timurid painting; Tabriz contributed to calligraphy the *nastaliq* script — and we must never forget that in Islamic countries calligraphy is considered the equal in importance of painting; but it was Herat that saw the finest flowering of the art of the book. Shah Rukh's library, and that formed by his son Baysunghur about 1420, must — to judge from what still survives — have been magnificent. Unfortunately Baysunghur, like so many of his family, took to the bottle and died when only in his early thirties, fourteen years before his father, of a fall after a dunken orgy.

Two things particularly strike the eye when looking at Timurid paintings: the incredible richness of their colour (a quality they share with Western medieval illuminated manuscripts) and their new concept of space. The craftsmanship of these artists is attested by the permanence of the brilliant colours that they used; the sense of space was achieved, as in Far Eastern painting, by the high horizon. The continued refusal to accept the Western convention of the cast and formed shadow resulted in the avoidance of those large areas of gloom, so characteristic of European oil paintings, which once provoked an Oriental to ask, 'What, do people in the West wash only one side of their faces?' The discarding of Western rules of perspective, which demand that distant objects be made smaller than foreground ones, allowed the whole picture space to be filled with incident.

Books needed to be bound; and here also, though Islamic binders turned for inspiration to the wooden bindings of the late Classical codices, Timurid craftsmen showed themselves masters

who surpassed contemporary European work in this field. The Persians (and the Turks, who were almost their equals in skill) did not use wood, preferring layers of varicoloured leather superimposed on pasteboard and filigreed to give almost the appearance of a cameo. Both the covers and the flap that protected the edges of the page were decorated. The tooling is often of almost unbelievable intricacy, and Emil Gratzl, writing in Upham Pope's *Survey*, discusses and reproduces a binding of 1434–35 in the Chester Beatty collection which has 550,000 blind stamps and 43,000 gold stamps – work which he estimates must have taken a good craftsman at least two years. Under the Safavids (after about 1525) bindings were of lacquer-painted *papier mâché*, often showing designs with animals and figures as complicated as those of the miniatures within.

Let us select one manuscript of the Timurid school of the first

Lacquer book cover showing a battle scene. Tabriz, Iran, sixteenth century.

OPPOSITE

'Paladins caught in a
blizzard.' From a
fifteenth-century
manuscript of the
epic Persian poem
Shah-nama.

half of the fifteenth century – a copy of Persia's great epic poem, Firdausi's *Shah-nama* or Book of Kings, written and illuminated about the year 1440 in Herat, which after passing through the hands of half a dozen Moghul emperors found a final resting-place in the library of the Royal Asiatic Society.

In this lovely book – clearly the work of several hands – are battle scenes, the storming of castles, and the mock battles of polo. One miniature shows that infant prodigy Rustam (who required ten wet-nurses to suckle him) slaying single-handed a white elephant. In another, a superb Chinese dragon, portrayed against a background of fantastic pink rocks which look like expensive bath salts, falls to the sword of the mighty Gushtasp. In a garden where hollyhocks and flowering shrubs do well, Firdausi himself is seen conversing with the court poets of Mahmud of Ghazni, while two men feed ducks and little Chinese clouds float by. Most unusual of all, perhaps, is the picture of the paladins caught in a blizzard, and there is also a memorable night scene.

The miniature chosen for reproduction illustrates a story popular from the earliest times – a story found embossed on Sassanian silver dishes and painted on twelfth-century pottery from Rayy: that of Bahram Gur and his favourite, Azada, at the chase. The maiden had challenged Bahram – 'that great hunter' – to perform various feats of prowess, the last being to transfix the ear and hoof of a buck with a single arrow. Bahram 'aimed an arrow at the ear of the buck, so that it grazed it, and it raised its hoof to scratch its ear. Then straightway he sent another arrow and pinned its foot and ear together.' For this brilliant feat Bahram expected Azada's praise; all he got was a snub. Understandably irritated, he flung the girl from the dromedary they were riding tandem and trampled her to death. 'And afterwards he would no more suffer damsels to go with him to the chase.' Nizami, in his *Khamsa* ('Five Poems'), has a variant of the story in which the girl is reported as having replied, 'Of course. Practice makes perfect!' In his version, however, the girl escaped death and by an ingenious stratagem eventually won back Bahram's favour.

This particular illustration is perhaps not entirely characteristic, in that the human interest is confined to a small part of the sheet. But the colour is exquisite – that rosy background would have appealed to Gauguin – and the enthusiastic, overburdened camel is marvellously realized. But characteristic certainly are the high horizon, the Chinese dragon-cloud, and the elegant tufts of flowers which refuse to diminish in size as they recede – all features that constantly recur in Timurid paintings.

A page from the same manuscript, showing Rustam and the siege of Gang-Bihisht, is more filled with incident. The fire that has breached the walls burns brightly, the catapult in the castle replies to the catapult and arrows of the besiegers, while from the windows of the castle peer apprehensive maidens who can be in no doubt as to the fate that awaits them if the city falls.

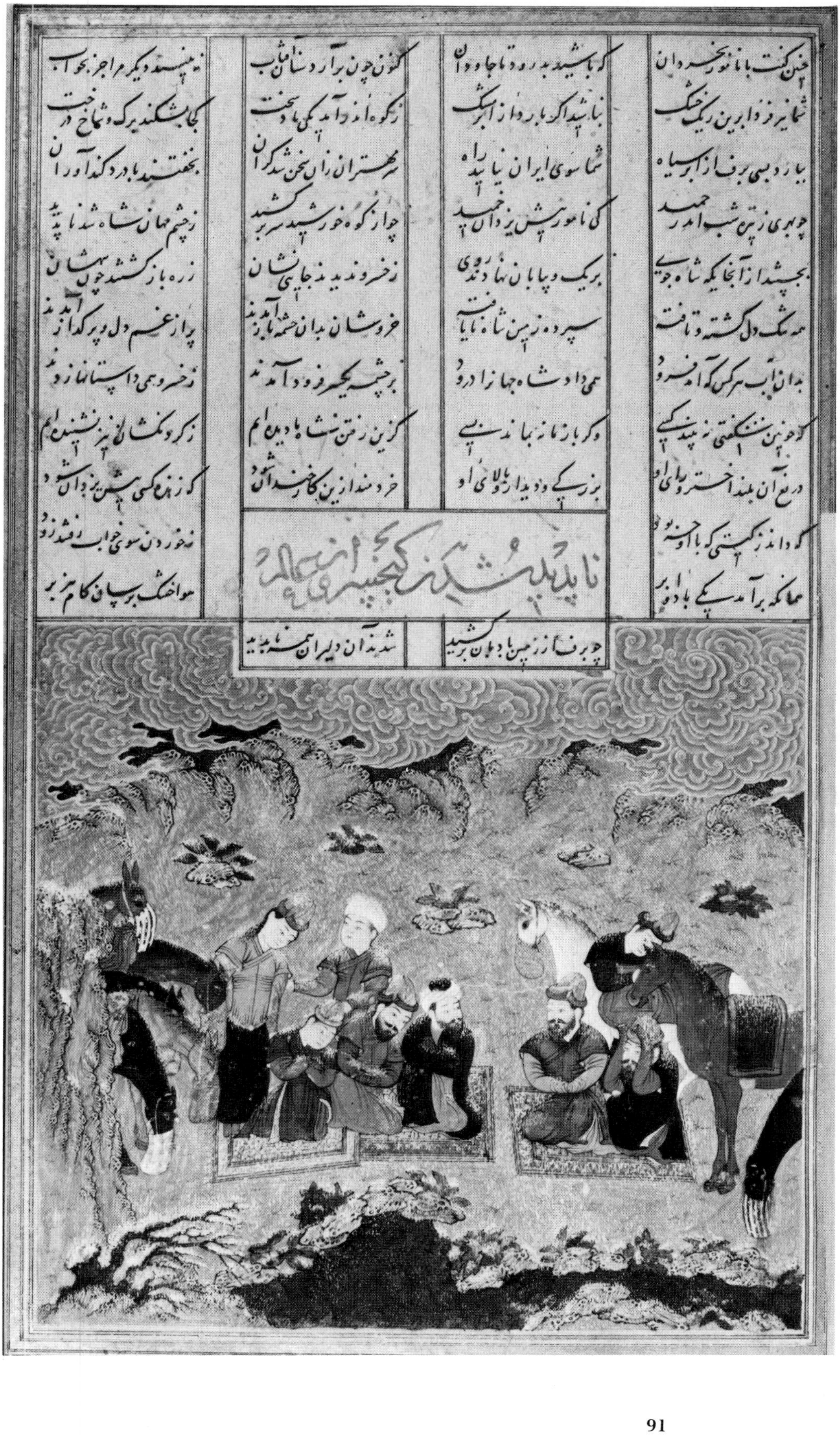
ناپدید شدن کیخسرو از عالم

The Timurids and the Art of the Book

The Shah Zinda, Samarkand, c. 1400. Detail of tilework in one of the mortuary chapels which cling to a hillside on the fringe of Samarkand.

In the middle of the fifteenth century the various descendents of Tamerlane were perpetually at one another's throats. Shah Rukh had died in 1447, and two years later Ulugh Beg was murdered by his own son. A great-grandson of Tamerlane, Abu Sa'id – another patron of scholars and artists – seized Samarkand in 1452 and gradually extended his authority over Transoxiana, Afghanistan and northern Persia; however, his callous murder of his octogenarian great-aunt, the spirited old Gauhar Shad, excuses us from shedding too many tears over his own assassination in 1468. He was succeed in Samarkand in turn by two of his own sons; but in Herat the power fell to another Timurid prince, Sultan Husayn, a great-great-grandson of Tamerlane, who ruled there as an independent monarch for nearly forty years (1468–1506).

'His was a wonderful age,' wrote Babur (1483–1530), the Timurid prince who was later to found the Moghul empire in India; 'the whole habitable world has not such a town as Herat had become under Sultan Husayn.' Babur – of whom more later – and his younger brother spent several weeks in Herat in the autumn of 1506, just after the death of the King, and left a valuable account of the life of the court there. Sultan Husayn he describes as cultured and talented, and in his youth manly and athletic – 'like a lion, slim from the waist down'; but 'when once he had in his hands a town like Herat, his only concern, by day and by night, was the pursuit of ease and pleasure.' It is to his old school friend and chief minister, Ali Shir Navoi, that we must turn to find the real promoter of this golden age.

'As a patron and protector of men of parts and accomplishments he had no equal,' wrote Babur. A wealthy bachelor with no family calls on his purse, he supported and encouraged promising musicians and poets (among the latter the famous Jami), and was largely responsible for drawing attention to the talents of a young artist named Bihzad, soon to become the most celebrated of all Persian miniature painters. But here, just where we might expect Babur to be informative, he lets us down; for his account of Bihzad is brief, indeed almost puerile: 'His work was very dainty, but he did not draw beardless faces well; he used to exaggerate the length of the double chin. But bearded faces he drew admirably.'

Where technique is concerned, Bihzad was not so much an innovator as a perfecter – a man who continued the tradition he had inherited, but who brought to it new subtlety and delicacy. Experts haggle, of course, over just which miniatures are the work of the master himself and which are by his pupils. Signatures avail little: some miniatures that bear his name are clearly not by him; others that are unsigned seem too good to be by anyone else. But his *style* is unmistakable, and probably, as with Rubens, the master sometimes applied a few finishing touches to the work of an assistant. Moreover, the Herat studio contained one or two artists – Mirak and Qasim Ali in particular – who approached him very closely.

The Timurids and the Art of the Book

PREVIOUS PAGES
LEFT

Hammam (bath-house) scene. Miniature from a manuscript of 1495 of the *Khamsa* (*Five-Poems*) of Nizami which has been attributed to Bihzad, the greatest Persian painter of his day.

RIGHT

'Bahram Gur and Azada at the chase.' From a manuscript of the *Shah-nama*, c. 1440.

A fine manuscript containing miniatures bearing the names of Bihzad, Mirak and Qasim Ali is a *Khamsa* of Nizami, dated 1495 and now in the British Museum. Dr Martin and Sir Thomas Arnold attributed eight paintings to Bihzad, while Mr Basil Gray, the leading authority in this country, considers that the *hammam* (bath-house) scene, chosen for our illustration, 'must preserve at least a composition from his hand.' Bihzad may not have been a technical innovator, but in this striking painting he reveals great originality of design.

It is, in fact, a double picture, showing two different rooms in the hammam. In one – the steam-bath – an attendant massages the head of a customer while other attendants fetch and carry pots of water; in the right-hand half of the design the bather's clothes lie on a couch on which he will in due course rest, and servants wring out wet towels. But what makes this scene unforgettable are the blue and green towels suspended high up near the ceiling. This is a brilliant touch and one which suggests a late eighteenth-century Japanese print, rather than a late fifteenth-century Persian miniature. Incidentally, if Bihzad is in fact the artist, the unbearded faces would seem to lend support to Babur's criticism.

Though Babur was deeply impressed by what he found at Herat, it was not primarily the cultural and artistic distinction of the city that had brought him there; he had gone to offer Sultan Husayn aid against a formidable threat of invasion by the Uzbek Turks, but finding that the King had died he decided that he was under no obligation to help the two rather unsatisfactory young princes who had succeeded him jointly. 'Ten dervishes may sleep under one blanket,' he quoted from Sa'adi's *Rose Garden*, 'but one country cannot contain two kings,' So Herat fell, and Babur, last of the Timurids, went on, as we shall see, to greater glory in India.

As for Bihzad, he seems to have remained for a time in Herat after the fall of the city; but four years later, when the young Shah Ismail, first of the great Safavid dynasty which was to rule Persia for two centuries, defeated the Uzbegs, Bihzad moved to Tabriz, the new capital.[1] Almost nothing is known of the later life of the artist beyond the fact that in 1522 he was put in charge of the royal workshop for the production of books. Here a whole team of specialists was employed – copyists, painters, gilders, margin-decorators, gold-beaters, gold-mixers, lapis-lazuli workers, binders and so on. It is very possible that administration increasingly occupied his time. Some interesting portraits – separate miniatures not associated with any book – bear his name; but these were much copied, and one cannot be sure whether any that survive are actually from his hand. Even the date of his death is not known, though it was probably about 1535. Some assert that he lived on in Tabriz until 1534, others that he died in 1524, the year that Shah Ismail was succeeded by the second Safavid ruler, Shah Tahmasp.

The Safavids

13

Throughout the second half of the fifteenth century Persia was in a state of confusion far too tangled to be unravelled here; but out of this chaos there eventually emerged a dynasty, the Safavid, which in the opinion of Sir Roger Stevens was 'more truly national than any since the Sassanians, and certainly comparable to it in splendour and renown.'

Its first monarch, a certain Ismail, was descended on his father's side from Ali, the Prophet's son-in-law, and a long line of devout men (*sufis*) established at Ardebil, near the Turkish border. But though Ismail had his fair share of the piety that ran in the family, he was not the man to allow it to stand in the way of his ambition; in 1499, when he was little more than a boy, he assembled a devoted little band of followers, seized Tabriz, then proclaimed himself Shah and proceeded to extend his territories eastwards where he defeated the Uzbegs at Balkh and Herat. A year later Isfahan and Shiraz fell to him; but the Uzbegs recovered Transoxiana, and for much of the rest of his reign he was chiefly occupied in warding off Turkish attacks from the north-west. He seems to have possessed charisma as well as talent: an Italian who saw him in the prime of youth described him as 'charming as a girl and lively as a fawn, left-handed, stronger than any of his lords, and at archery able to hit the apple six time out of ten'. More, indeed, than charisma; for his soldiers, convinced of the power of his sanctity, are said to have (rather rashly?) gone into battle unarmed. He is still gratefully remembered in Iran for having established the Shi'ite doctrines as the national religion.

Ismail's son Tahmasp, who was only ten years old when he succeeded his father in 1524, sensibly moved his capital to Kazvin so as to be at a safer distance from the ever troublesome Turks. It was during Tahmasp's long reign of fifty-one years that the European powers, clutching gratefully at any possible, even unholy, alliance that might give them support against the Turks, began to make friendly overtures to the Persians. This led in due course to a remarkable *rapprochement* which reached its peak in the glorious reign of the fifth and most illustrious of the Safavids, Shah Abbas the Great (1587–1629), to whose capital, Isfahan, there flocked a whole host of admiring ambassadors, merchants, missionaries, sightseers and adventurers. And it is to Isfahan that the traveller today, eager to see why it is that so many people have fallen in love with Islamic architecture, should turn for the most easily accessible and immediately rewarding prospect of the splendours of Iranian tilework, turquoise domes and lofty minarets.

Throughout the seventeenth century, Isfahan continued to dazzle European visitors, many of whom left detailed accounts of what they found there. Then, in 1722, came the Afghans who captured and looted the city, to be followed a decade later by the last of the great Asiatic conquerors, Nadir Kuli, who proclaimed himself Shah and finally extinguished, after more than two centuries, the enfeebled Safavids. Meshed now became the capital, and Isfahan, licking her many wounds, relapsed for ever into a provincial town of small political importance.

It was, as we shall see, the minor arts that flourished most vigorously under the first Safavids, and much of what they built has perished. But in Isfahan the portals of the mausoleum of Harun Vilayet and the mosque of Ali give more than a taste of the magical quality of Persian tilework in Shah Ismail's day. There is probably no important building assignable to the long reign of Shah Tahmasp; the palace and mosque that he built at Kazvin, his caravanserai near Sultaniya and his various summer residences are no more. This was in part the result of the reckless use of unfired bricks. But the lovely tilework in the south-west ivan of the Friday Mosque in Isfahan still survives — sad reminder of the quality of what has been lost to us elsewhere.

Shah Abbas, when he ascended the throne in 1587, was fortunate enough to find that one of Persia's two most dangerous enemies, the Turks, were too occupied waging war in Hungary to present any immediate threat to his kingdom; he therefore attacked and trounced that other recurrent pest, the Uzbegs. But the Turks might at any time be free to return, and his capital, Kazvin, was still uncomfortably near the Turkish border. So his thoughts turned to creating a new one elsewhere, and Isfahan seemed exactly to meet his requirements.

Isfahan was the capital of the province and ancient kingdom of Fars (from which the word 'Persia' is derived) — a town with a long history and of a certain importance, fairly centrally situated, with a good climate and considerable reserves of water not far below ground. As we have already seen, it possessed a magnificent Friday Mosque, and it was to be further embellished by Abbas's successors; but if ever a city could be described as a creation of a single man, that city was Isfahan and that man Shah Abbas the Great.

A French diplomat, Abel Pinçon, has described Abbas as he appeared in 1599, when at the age of about twenty-eight he was starting on the grandiose plan that was to make Isfahan one of the most splendid cities of the world of his day. Pinçon says that he was short and well built, good-looking, with black hair and beard and big mustachios that drooped a little because it was presump-

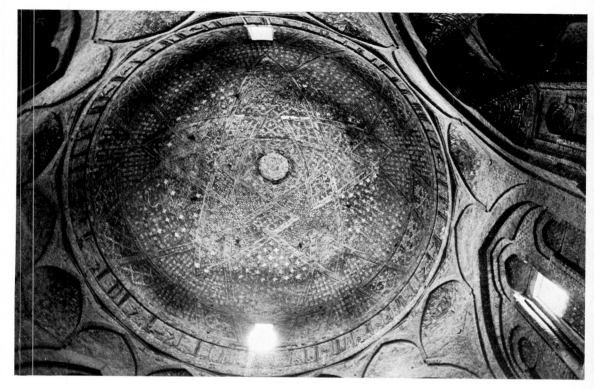

tuous to train them heavenwards. A Carmelite adds that he was
'bright-witted, martial, mercurial, strong, skilful, healthy,
resolute, with a good memory and a sagacious in business'. He
mixed freely with his subjects and was in general amiable to the
foreigners who flocked to his court. That he was also a lecher, a
sodomite, and on occasions a butcher goes almost without saying.

What he achieved in Isfahan may fairly be described as town-
planning. A magnificent bridge, the Allahverdi Khan (or Thirty-
three-arch Bridge) leads from the river (the Zayandeh-rud) by
way of a broad and shady avenue (the Chahar Bagh) to the palace
grounds, beyond which is a vast open rectangular space (the
Maidan) used in Shah Abbas's day for polo, archery, animal combats, a weekly market, public hangings and other similar enter-
tainments. Commanding the Maidan on the palace side is a
pavilion gateway (the Ali Qapu, or Sublime Porte) with a terrace
where the Shah entertained distinguished guests or used as a
grandstand to watch the polo when he himself was not playing. At
one end of the Maidan stands the Masjid-i-Shah (Royal Mosque),
at the other the entrance to the bazars, while opposite to the Ali
Qapu comes the smaller Lutfullah Mosque erected by the Shah in
honour of a shaikh of that name to whom writers always refer as
his 'saintly father-in-law'.

'Let me lead you,' wrote Sir Thomas Herbert,[1] 'into the
Maidan . . . without doubt as spacious, as pleasant and aromatic
a market as any in the universe.' This is still a magnificent square,
perhaps the largest and the finest in the world, enclosed by
double-tiered, white-and-blue arcades punctuated at intervals

[1] *Some Yeares Travaile*, 1634.

99

The Shaikh
Lutfullah Mosque,
Isfahan, the building
of which was started
in 1603.

by splendid buildings. Today the centre of it has been turned into a formal garden with a pool, summer bedding and western-style seats – agreeable enough, proper enough in Europe, but sadly out of character here. Lucky are those who saw it forty years ago!

The Ali Qapu had been a little Timurid palace, and probably the reconstruction of it was Abbas's first task. The result is frankly rather comical, and Robert Byron's famous jibe – 'that brick boot-box' – has some justification. Inside are the remains of murals which, according to the prim Italian traveller Pietro Della Valle, 'show men and women in lascivious postures', but which would not today bring a blush to the cheeks of even the most maiden of aunts. On the top floor is a music room whose walls and ceiling are curiously pierced, as if fretsawed, in the shapes of flagons and wine vessels – perhaps to improve the acoustics.

The Lutfullah Mosque, begun in 1603, is an enchantingly

beautiful little building with a squat dome of unglazed *café-au-lait* tiles laced with arabesques of glazed white, turquoise and ultramarine. Inside, the tilework is of incredible intricacy. As Byron says, Versailles, the porcelain rooms at Schönbrunn, the Doge's Palace, and St Peter's, are rich, but this surpasses them all in sheer exuberance of decoration.

The Royal Mosque was begun a decade later, and Shah Abbas, fearing that his time was running out (he was right; it remained unfinished at his death), drove his architects too hard. The result was shoddy foundations and the use of so-called *haft-rangi* (seven coloured) square tiles in place of a true mosaic of cut self-coloured tiles. This halves the labour but slightly diminishes the brilliance. Byron savagely attacked the Royal Mosque, whose 'huge blue bulk and huge acreage of coarse floral tilework' constituted in his opinion 'just that kind of "oriental" scenery so dear to the Omar Khayyam fiends – pretty, if you like, even magnificent, but not important in the general scale of things'. But – *pace* Byron – the overall effect is staggering. Of course the Lutfullah and the dome chambers of the Friday Mosque are *purer*; but to those who cannot get to Meshed, there is nothing in all Iran that gives a better idea of the sumptuousness of Iranian architecture than the towering entrance portal and immense turquoise dome of the Masjid-i-Shah.

Inside the palace grounds is the Chihil Sutun, an elegant ceremonial palace possibly begun in Shah Abbas's time but at all events much altered subsequently. The name means 'forty columns'; in fact the *talar* (open audience hall) has only twenty, and it is often said that the reflection of these in the pool produces the required number. However, 'forty' is commonly used in Persian and Arabic for a large but imprecise number (Ali Baba and his *forty* thieves), and the 'reflection' theory, though picturesque enough to be oriental, is no more than an ingenious occidental invention. The building is now a museum.

The Allahverdi Khan Bridge, which connects Isfahan with the Armenian suburb of Julfa, is three hundred yards long and a noble piece of engineering; but many people will find the Khwaju Bridge, built in the time of Shah Abbas II (*c.* 1650), the more attractive, its six semi-octagonal pavilions relieving the monotony which mars the other. The Khwaju is at once a bridge and a dam, and in Safavid times was the evening resort of the Isfahanis and the scene of annual water festivals which were considered failures unless a fair number of the participants were drowned.

Lord Curzon considered the mosque and madrasa of the Mother of the Shah, built by Shah Sultan Husain in the Chahar Bagh in the opening years of the eighteenth century, 'one of the stateliest ruins' in all Persia, and Upham Pope that it was 'the last construction that in any sense deserves the qualification "great"'. Since Curzon's day it has, like much else in Isfahan, been admirably restored. Its court, planted with majestic *chenars* (oriental plane trees) is one of the most picturesque in the city. The adjoining

The Khwaju Bridge, Isfahan, c. 1650. It serves both as a bridge and as a dam.

caravanserai, which once provided the money for the upkeep of the madrasa, is now the luxury Shah Abbas Hotel.

Then, in 1722, came the Afghans. . . .

However, though the great days of Persian architecture were over, there is in various parts of the country much else of a later date which gives pleasure. In Shiraz, for example, which continued to flourish after Isfahan waned, there is the handsome Vakil Mosque (1773), described by Roger Stevens as 'the only major example of ecclesiastical architecture in Iran dating from the second half of the eighteenth century'.

Moreover, today the architecture and painting of the early years of the Qajar dynasty (1787–1925) have suddenly become fashionable in the West, much as have Victorian things in England. At Mahan, beyond Kerman on the fringes of the formidable Dasht-i-Lut desert, is a much-loved shrine in an exquisite setting: that of a saint named Nasreddin Nimatullah, who died in 1431. Begun soon after the saint's death, it dates from many periods. Shah Abbas enlarged it, but it was the Qajars who, by adding a second pair of minarets and much of their favourite pink and yellow tilework, have left the strongest mark upon it. As architecture it is unimportant; but its pools and its cypresses, its umbrella pines and its riot of single white roses, its backcloth of lavender mountains, its cool and its shade and its silence, make it a magical spot. Nimatullah was a prophet as well as a saint, and in such a place prophecy must come easily. He foretold, amongst other things, that in 1857 the 'Franks' would be driven out of India. He might so easily have been right.

The Minor Arts under the Safavids

14

There is no difficulty in choosing a manuscript to represent the early Safavid period, though which of its miniatures to select for reproduction is a problem indeed. The volume is a *Khamsa* of Nizami, written and illustrated in Tabriz between 1539 and 1543 for Shah Tahmasp and described by that great pioneer of the study of Persian miniatures, Dr F. R. Martin, as 'the finest sixteenth-century manuscript in existence'.[1] This sumptuous folio was acquired by the British Museum in 1880 for two thousand pounds – a considerable sum in those days; but never was money better spent. The names of five different artists are to be found on the miniatures, and though these are not signatures there is little reason to doubt the attributions. Nonetheless, the level of performance is so consistently high, and the technique in all the paintings so similar, that it would not be difficult to accept them as the work of a single artist.

The best known and most frequently reproduced of the miniatures is probably that showing the ascent of the Prophet to heaven – a dazzlingly beautiful treatment of the theme. No artist's name is attached to this, nor to the 'Physicians' duel' which illustrates an amusing episode in the first of the five poems. Two rival doctors have challenged one another to a fight to the death, using as weapons only their professional skills. The first had given the second a deadly bolus to swallow; but he instantly recognized its ingredients and took an antidote that rendered it 'as harmless as a lump of sugar'. The picture shows the second act of the drama. The doctor whose turn it now is plucks a rose, breathes a spell upon it and offers it to his opponent to smell. But the wretched man, knowing of nothing in his pharmacopoea to counteract magic, drops dead of fright. Another splendid miniature, 'Majnun in the desert' by Mirak, shows the disconsolate young lover fraternizing with a variety of wild beasts (the lion, we are told, offered his services as a pillow) in what looks like a very well run nature reserve.

But we have chosen to reproduce 'Shirin bathing' – possibly the most subtle in colour of all the miniatures. Against a golden sky with scudding 'Chinese' clouds is patterned the loveliest oriental plane in all Persian art. Among rocks of ochre, pale lavender and aquamarine rides Prince Khosru on a lavender steed, gazing with admiration at the maiden who, as the result of the oxydisation of the silver paint, appears to be sitting on a stretch of tarmac rather than bathing in water.

[1] Excellent colour reproductions of its fourteen principal paintings (several inferior ones were added a century later) were published by *The Studio* in 1928 with a description by Laurence Binyon.

The Minor Arts under the Safavids

As the sixteenth century drew to its close, painting became to a large extent dissociated from the illustration of manuscripts, and we find a number of separate miniatures showing portraits of men, dancers and courtesans. At the same time mural painting was revived, and many examples can be seen on the walls of the palaces in Isfahan.

The greatest name among the miniature painters, a name second only to that of Bihzad, is Riza-i-Abbasi – an elusive man indeed! Many thousands of words, chiefly by Germans who take kindly to this kind of detective work, have been written about him; but the mystery still remains. Was he the same as Aqa Riza? Were there *two* Aqa Rizas? Where does Aqa Muhammad Riza fit in? Was Riza-i-Abbasi the father of Shafi Abbasi? And so on. Somebody once put forward the theory that Shakespeare's works were not written by Shakespeare but by another man of the same name, and one might reasonably postulate a similar theory about the paintings of Riza-i-Abbasi. A good working hypothesis is that there were two artists – first Aqa Riza, and then Riza-i-Abbasi.

Mass vestment, now mutilated, of silk and gold and silver thread, made probably in Isfahan in the early seventeenth century for the Armenian colony in New Julfa.

104

It seems likely that Aqa Riza was the son of a Meshed court official, and that about 1590 a portrait by him attracted the attention of Shah Abbas who, when he had dealt with the Uzbegs, summoned him to Isfahan. It is said that towards 1608 Aqa Riza grew idle and frittered away his time watching wrestling, and most of his best paintings probably date from the closing decade of the sixteenth century. If it is difficult to make precise identification of his work, his style is at all events easily recognizable. Many of his paintings show single figures in mannered postures and languid attitudes. Often they sway a little forwards, knees slightly bent, in rhythms that curiously recall the ivory carvings of medieval Europe. The shoulders slope, the contour of the cheek is full as an infant's and the lips part in a wistful smile.

Riza-i-Abbasi was a dazzling draughtsman whose fluid, mannered line, with its thickening accents and spluttered termination, has the calligraphic brilliance which we associate with the work of Far Eastern artists; and no doubt there is direct influence through the Chinese artisans whom Abbas had summoned to his capital. Riza-i-Abbasi often worked in monochrome

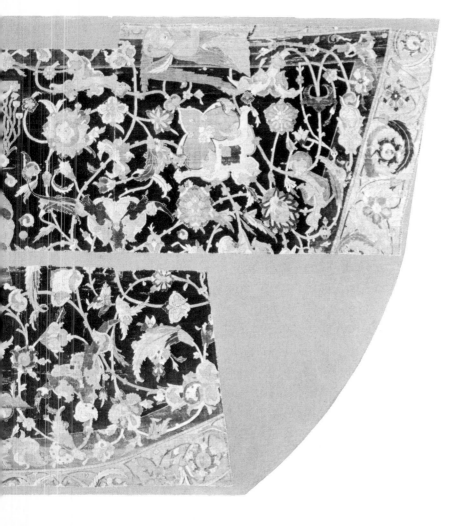

RIGHT

Miniature painting
of instrumentalists,
sixteenth-century
Persian.

OPPOSITE

The Blue Mosque
1609–16, Istanbul,
Turkey. Built for
Sultan Ahmed I by a
pupil or follower of
Sinan, Turkey's
greatest architect.

OVERLEAF LEFT

'Khusrau's elephants
trample on the
enemy.' Miniature
attributed to Riza-i-
Abbasi, seventeenth
century.

OVERLEAF RIGHT

'Shirin bathing.'
From a *Khamsa* of
Nizami, written and
illustrated in Tabriz
between 1539 and
1543 for Shah
Tahmasp. This is
generally considered
the finest of all
surviving sixteenth-
century Persian
manuscripts.

heightened with gold, and his *oeuvre* includes portraits of Europeans and also erotic subjects. He may have died in 1635.

Iran, since the earliest days of her history, had been famous for her rich fabrics. Clothes were sumptuous; garden pavilions were hung with gorgeous materials; horses were superbly caparisoned. There were magnificent banners for use in war and in tournaments, and wonderful curtains and cushions in private houses; and it is amusing to note that, as early as at least the fifteenth century, door-curtains were looped back with sashes, a style later to become fashionable in the West. On state occasions the roads were covered, sometimes for miles, with brocades, cloth of gold and embroideries. Much of this traditional splendour is represented in the miniatures of the fifteenth, sixteenth and seventeenth centuries.

With the establishment of the Safavid dynasty craftsmen from eastern Iran and Transoxiana moved westwards, and in Isfahan in the seventeenth century woven fabrics achieved an opulence that was never to be surpassed. The output of brocades, taffetas, velvets and compound twill with metal thread ground, must have been enormous, and some idea of their incredible richness, delicacy and range can be gauged from the plates in Professor Pope's *Survey* and from numerous examples in the Victoria and Albert Museum.

The Rugs of Islam

The origin of the clipped pile (as opposed to the woven) carpet has long been a matter of speculation. That famous Orientalist and classical scholar Sir George Birdwood 'delved, with characteristic zeal, into the ancient writers for proofs of the existence of pile carpets in the time of Cyrus – who died in 529 B.C. He quoted in support of his thesis from the Bible and from scores of classical writers. . . . There are references in plenty to vestments, hangings, draperies, brocades and embroidered cloths; but there is no reference which can be construed as indicating that pile carpets were in use in Achaemenian times.'[1] He concluded that we do not know, and in all probability never shall, whether the floors of the palace of Darius at Persepolis were covered with pile or merely with woven carpets.

However, the relatively recent discovery, in a natural 'deep freeze' at Pazyryk in the Altai mountains of southern Siberia, of a magnificent pile carpet in almost perfect condition and dating from about the fourth century B.C., has changed everything. The horses on the outer border so closely resemble those carved on one of the staircases at Persepolis that it is difficult to doubt that this carpet was made in Iran. Thus it would seem that Birdwood may well have been right after all.

In any case, pile carpets (qali) were undoubtedly being made by nomads in Iran, Iraq and Anatolia long before the days of Islam. But since they were intended for the most part for use – and *hard* use – on the ground, very little has come down to us which can be dated with any probability earlier than about the year 1400. Another alleged cause of their disappearance is more curious. It is said that the Turks, mystified by the high prices paid by Europeans for worn-out carpets, concluded that they possessed the secret of turning them into gold, and so destroyed many in a vain attempt to discover how this was done.

In fact, one of our best sources of information for the appearance of early rugs, Anatolian in particular, is the representation of them in contemporary European paintings[2] and Persian miniatures. Several of such rugs, probably Turkish, have, however, survived; one found in a church in Central Italy is now in Berlin and another from a village church in Sweden is in the Historical Museum in Stockholm. Both these show two octagonal panels containing stylized animals, and probably date from about 1400. Others from Anatolian mosques have been tentatively

OPPOSITE

The Ardebil Carpet, 1539. One of the largest, and probably the most famous carpet in the world.

OVERLEAF LEFT

An outstanding silk rug from Kashan.

OVERLEAF RIGHT

Persian prayer rug, seventeenth century.

[1] A. C. Edwards in *The Legacy of Persia*, ed. by A. J. Arberry, Oxford University Press, 1953.

[2] For example, the 'Annunciation' of Carlo Crivelli (1430?–93?) and 'The Ambassadors' of Hans Holbein the younger (1497–1543), both in the National Gallery, London.

113

attributed to the thirteenth century, and there is a fresco of 1259
in a church near Sofia which shows St Nicholas buying from a
poor man what looks very like a pile rug.

The finest Persian carpets – which means, of course, the finest
carpets in the world – were made under the Safavids, the peak
being reached in the long reign of Shah Tahmasp and sustained
until the death of Shah Abbas in 1629. Tahmasp was greatly
interested in carpets, and is said to have designed a few himself.
He is also on record as having written to his arch-enemy, Suleiman the Magnificent, offering to make him the diplomatic gift of
carpets for his new mosque in Istanbul (see page 121) and telling
him not forget to give the required sizes; these were duly dis-
patched and safely received.

Edwards has made his personal choice of the seven greatest
surviving carpets, all of which date from between about 1520 and
the early years of the seventeenth century; and we in England are
fortunate indeed that of these seven, three are in the Victoria and
Albert Museum in London, among them the Ardebil carpet – by
general consent the noblest of them all.[1] In the very limited space
at our disposal we may perhaps be allowed to concentrate our
attention upon the history of this masterpiece.

This carpet was one of a pair presented to the mosque in Ardebil,
where Shah Ismail and his pious ancestors were buried, by Ismail's
son Shah Tahmasp. It is remarkable for its tranquil, abstract
beauty (no men or animals could figure in a carpet destined for a
mosque), for its immense size (about 35 feet by 18 feet, with over
thirty million knots) and for the unusual (though not unique)
inclusion of a cartouche bearing a name, a date, and a couple of
lines of Hafiz:

> I have no refuge in the world other than thy threshold;
> There is no protection for my head other than this door.

> The work of the slave of the threshold,
> Maqsud Kashani, in the year 946   [A.D. 1539].

But where was it made, and what part did Maqsud of Kashan
play in its manufacture? Kurt Erdmann, in *Seven Hundred Years
of Oriental Carpets*, suggests that he was probably the head
of the workshop where it was woven, and that he would not
have mentioned that he was 'of Kashan' had he been working
there. As to the place of its origin, Tabriz, Kazvin and Ardebil
itself have all been tentatively suggested.

For more than three centuries the two carpets lay on the floor
of the Ardebil Mosque, trodden daily by the bare feet of hundreds
of worshippers. But in the 1880s the authorities, finding themselves in need of a substantial sum of money for the repair of the
fabric, decided to sell some of their rugs, and thus these two huge

[1] The others in that collection are the 'Chelsea'
carpet and a 'Vase'
carpet with a red ground.
Of the remainder, two
are in Vienna, one in
Milan and one in New
York.

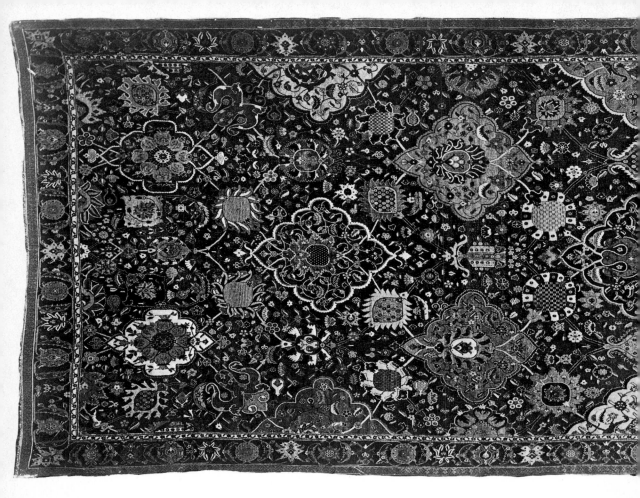

Persian woollen carpet, sixteenth to seventeenth centuries.

and rather damaged pieces passed in 1888 to the London firm of Messrs V. J. Robinson. For several years nothing was heard of them; then, one day in 1892, the public was invited to see a single carpet – the finest in the world, and in a state of 'perfect preservation'. The price asked was the at that time enormous sum of two thousand five hundred pounds, which no museum anywhere could then afford. However, an appeal launched by Sir A. W. Franks and William Morris was so successful that in the following year the Victoria and Albert Museum was able to acquire it.

What the public did not know (though the Director of the Museum of course did) was that Robinson had bought *both* rugs, and that the apparently perfectly preserved piece sold in 1893 was in fact an amalgam of the two, much of the border of the more damaged rug having been skilfully and laboriously used to repair the other. For a time the mutilated piece was concealed; but eventually it was sold to an American collector on condition that it was never shown in England. Sir Joseph Duveen acquired it in 1919, and in 1931, the ban having by then been lifted, it was displayed in the great Persian Exhibition at Burlington House. Later it was bought by Mr Paul Getty, and is now in the County Museum, Los Angeles. 'It is true it is a ruin,' writes Erdmann, 'but, when washed, brilliant in its depth of colouring and therefore almost superior to its big brother in the Victoria and Albert Museum which is too big to be washed.' In 1975, however, the

latter carpet was taken to Birmingham (where the water is softer than London's) and successfully washed for two days on a sloping platform – an operation that was filmed. Repairs are now in hand, and it is expected that it will be on view again in 1976.

London's Ardebil carpet, astonishing though it is, may be considered by some as too subdued, too abstract, and too overwhelming. For those who prefer incident and brighter colours there are the great hunting carpets, of which that in the Kunstgewerbe Museum in Vienna, originally a treasure of the imperial house of Austria, is probably the most remarkable. It dates from the middle of the sixteenth century, and warp, weft and pile are all of pure silk. It was no doubt designed by one of the miniature painters who worked for Shah Tahmasp, for it shows a stupendous royal hunt such as is figured in a painting by Sultan Muhammad in the already discussed *Khamsa* of Nizami of 1539–43.

In Shah Abbas's time a royal carpet factory was established in Isfahan in the palace grounds just behind the Ali Qapu, and another great centre of manufacture is said to have been at Joshaqan Qali ('Joshaqan the carpet–[town]'), about sixty-five miles to the north-west of the capital. Here in 1661 were made the magnficent floral carpets for the tomb-chamber of Shah Abbas II at Qum. Many carpets were also made in Kashan.

The carpets made for Abbas the Great were, as one would expect, large and grandoise. The 'vase' carpets – also, and more

Detail of the Persian 'Hunting Carpet', probably mid-sixteenth century and now in Vienna.

reasonably, called 'Shah Abbas' carpets – contain great palmettes, huge leaves, flower-strewn meadows, and sometimes animals. The 'Polonaise' carpets, many of them made as gifts to European princes, were enriched with threads of silk, gold-covered silver, and silver. They were used to cover floors and tables or to decorate walls; and the French jeweller Tavernier tells us that the royal hunting cheetahs were privileged to lie on them. In the Victoria and Albert Museum is a remarkable chasuble made of a silk carpet with, in the centre, a representation of the Crucifixion; this was no doubt executed at Abbas's command for the Armenians of Julfa, with whom he was often on the friendliest of terms.

From Persia and Anatolia the craft of carpet-making spread throughout the world. It was probably introduced into India in the fourteenth century, but not extensively developed there until the days of the Mughals. In Spain a few rugs clearly inspired by Anatolian models survive from the period immediately preceding the conquest of Granada, and it is very possible that it was Moriscos who continued to operate the looms after the Muslims had been driven out. The great carpet factories of England and France date from the seventeenth century.

In Iran and those countries who share a common border with her the tribal rug continues to flourish, and carpet-making remains, in spite of mechanization, a sturdy cottage industry in the lands of Islam.

The Ottoman Turks

The year 1453 is one that 'every schoolboy knows', for it witnessed an event of enormous importance in the history of Europe – the fall of Constantinople to the Ottoman (or Osmanli)[1] Turks and thus the end, after more than eleven centuries, of the Eastern Roman Empire.

It was in 1227 that several thousand of these Central Asian refugees, fleeing before the advancing Mongols, had made their first appearance in Antolia, where the Seljuk Ala ad-Din (see page 42), after some initial reluctance, allowed them to settle near Ankara. He had no cause to regret this generous gesture, for his guests continued to help him against the Mongols. But the days of the Seljuks were already numbered, and in the fourteenth century the Ottomans gradually gained control of a large part of western Islam; with the capture of Constantinople by Muhammad II (ruled 1451–81) they became masters of an empire that was to endure until the proclamation of the Republic in 1923.

It may be counted a piece of good fortune for Ottoman architects that they inherited in Constantinople (henceforth Stamboul or Istanbul) one of the noblest buildings ever erected in Christendom – the Church of Santa Sophia, built for Justinian by Greek architects in the sixth century. 'Glory be to God who has considered me worthy to accomplish such a work!' cried the Emperor when, on 27 December 537, the solemn inauguration took place; and boastfully, yet perhaps truthfully, he added, 'O Solomon, I have surpassed you!' For nine centuries Santa Sophia was a Christian church, for nearly five a mosque; then in 1935, as a part of Atatürk's campaign to launch Turkey into the modern world, this building in which unnumbered millions had worshipped was turned into a museum.

A thousand years after Justinian there emerged in Istanbul another Greek architect who was to achieve international fame: Sinan (1489–1588). The son of a Christian stonemason from the high Anatolian plateau, at the age of twenty-three young Sinan was conscripted by the Janissaries of Selim the Grim and enrolled in the Turkish army. Here his skill at bridge-building was brought to the notice of the Sultan, who in due course appointed him court architect – a post he continued to hold under Selim's successors Suleiman the Magnificent, Selim the Sot and Murad III. Sinan's industry was immense, and since he was still in harness at the age of ninety-seven his output was enormous. To

[1] So called from Osman (in Arabic, Othman), one of their early leaders and first Sultan (c. 1299–1326).

him have been attributed no less than eighty-one large mosques and fifty-one smaller ones, together with innumerable libraries, palaces, hammams, aquaducts, mausoleums, caravanserais and fountains, many of which have of course vanished over the years. By general consent the Suleimaniyé Mosque in Istanbul (1550-55) and the Selimiyé Mosque at Adrianople (now Edirné) built about 1570, are his masterpieces. Sinan is reported to have said that the former showed him to be competent, the latter that he was a master; but both, of course, reveal how much he owed to the incomparable masterpiece of Santa Sophia.

Suleiman was worthy of the splendid building that bears his name, for it was in his reign that Ottoman power reached its zenith. In 1526 the flower of Hungarian chivalry was annihilated at the battle of Mohács; three years later the Turks were at the gates of Vienna, and at the time of Suleiman's death in 1566 his empire included Algeria and Egypt and extended from the borders of Germany to those of Persia.

The Suleimaniyé, with its spreading, dove-grey dome and elegant needle-like minarets, follows a pattern familiar throughout Turkey. Within, the vast space is flooded by light that comes from many windows high up in the building, while once it was lit at night by more than twenty thousand lamps. A certain Evliya Chelebi,[1] a seventeenth-century Turkish globe-trotter, records seeing 'ten Frankish infidels skilful in geometry and architecture' – probably Italians who had managed to gain access to the Suleimaniyé – so overwhelmed that they 'tossed their hats into the air and, crying "Mother of God!"' continued on their way bareheaded. 'Each of the ten bit his finger in astonishment, that being their manner of testifying the greatest amazement.' Asked what they thought of the building, one replied, 'Nowhere is there so much beauty, external and internal, to be found united', and added that in the whole of Frangistan (Christian Western Europe) there was not a single edifice to compare with it. Had they, one wonders, seen St Peter's; had they, indeed, forgotten Santa Sophia?

But the Selimiyé at Adrianople is indubitably finer than the Suleimaniyé. Here, wrote Grube, 'the final solution [of roofing such a building] is achieved by putting the columns that support the huge central dome so close to the walls . . . that they seem to become part of them,' thus creating 'an enormous floating dome over a unified, intensely light room'. A legend states that the mosque was built on the site of a tulip garden whose proud owner, an elderly woman, long refused to sell her land, but who finally consented on condition that the bulbs were replanted elsewhere and that she and her tulips were recorded for all time in the mosque. As evidence of the truth of this story, the guide draws the attention of visitors to an inverted tulip carved on one of the columns. The Ottomans adopted the tulip as the emblem of their house.

OPPOSITE

Istanbul. Interior of the Suleimaniyé Mosque, 1550–55.

OVERLEAF LEFT

'Youth dancing with a musical instrument.' Persian miniature in the style of Aqa Riza, c. 1600.

OVERLEAF RIGHT

Detail of a Qajar mural painting of a girl with clasped hands, c. 1800.

Narrative of Travels Oriental Translation Fund, London, 1834, 1846.

Incidentally, it was near Adrianople in the year 1554 that Busbecq, ambassador from Ferdinand of Austria to Suleiman the Magnificent, observed 'an abundance of flowers . . . which the Turks call *tulipam*. . . . I received several presents of these flowers, which cost me not a little.' This is the first definite reference in Western literature to the tulip. As to its name, the Turkish word for the flower is *lalé*, and it seems probable that Busbecq misunderstood his interpreter when he compared the shape of its petals to that of a turban (*dulban*).

In the seventeenth century further important mosques were erected in Turkey, the most impressive and the largest being that of Sultan Ahmed I, built in Istanbul between 1609 and 1616 by an architect who followed closely in Sinan's footsteps and who was probably his pupil. So keen was Ahmed to see his mosque (often called the Blue Mosque) completed that he is said to have worked alongside his men – something which today would no doubt have precipitated a general strike. He was determined that it should surpass Santa Sophia, and in fact its dome is both wider and higher than that of its prototype. Until the end of the eighteenth century its two hundred and sixty windows were filled with stained glass, and much of the mystery vanished when this was removed. Today a couple of Victorian grandfather clocks stand guard over its entrance.

Everybody must be familiar with the glorious prospect of Istanbul as viewed across the water, with the dome of Santa Sophia dominating the hill that crowns Seraglio Point. The Grand Seraglio (Topkapi Sarayi) is a town in itself, and until the fall of the Ottomans its inner courts were as impenetrable by infidels as was the Potala at Lhasa. Perhaps in all those years not more than a dozen Christians had ever passed beyond the Gate of Felicity into the Third Court, and even as late as 1926 Sir George Young could write that 'up till now the Seraglio Hareem and the Hirkai Sherif Odassi [Pavilion of the Holy Mantle] remain two of the very few places on earth that no Anglo-Saxon or American foot has as yet trod. As the Pole used to be for explorers – as Everest still is for mountaineers – so have the Sultan's Hareem and the Hirkai Sherif been for tourists.'

Today Everest has been conquered – though not yet converted into a tourist attraction; but virtually the whole of the Topkapi Sarayi is now easier of access to the public than is Buckingham Palace. The buildings within this walled city – its gates, throne room and treasury, its library, baths, pavilions and kiosks – are not 'great' architecture; but many of them are charming, and in the museum may be seen a vast number of *objets d'art* of every conceivable kind including a fabulous collection of some ten thousand pieces of Chinese porcelain. The Topkapi Sarayi also houses many splendid Persian and Turkish manuscripts and, for the faithful, a piece of the Prophet's beard and one of the four

OPPOSITE

Fatehpur Sikri, India. The Boland Darwaza ('Lofty Gateway'), 1569–72. The Emperor Akbar built this now deserted city near Agra to be his capital, but probably because of poor water supplies it was soon abandoned.

Sultans of the
Ottoman dynasty.

LEFT TO RIGHT

Muhammad II,
1451–81; Selim II,
1566–74; Bayazid I,
1389–1403 and
Murad II, 1421–51.
Miniatures from a
Turkish manuscript,
c. 1600.

teeth knocked from his mouth by a blow from a battle-axe at the battle of Bedr.

In the Chinili (or Tile) Kiosk and elsewhere in the Topkapi Sarayi may be seen wonderful examples of Turkish polychrome tilework. The industry was started in the fifteenth century and reached its peak of perfection in the sixteenth. Here the Turkish love of flowers is everywhere apparent, and the tulip panels in the bedroom of the feeble Murad III (1574–95) are particularly lovely. Bursa (Brusa), in Asia Minor, also has splendid tilework to show. The so-called 'Rhodian' pottery, whose plates and jars are well known in the West, was in fact made in the court factory at Isnik, the ancient Nicaea.

Ottoman painting is a subject still needing further study. Tabriz was more than once in Ottoman hands in the sixteenth century, and Far Eastern elements which had reached that city by way of Herat are apparent in a fine drawing of a dragon, at one time the property of Charles Shannon but now in the Cleveland Museum of Art. Grube reproduces a curious page from a manuscript of Firdausi's *Suleiman-nama* (Book of King Solomon) of about 1500, mysteriously describing it as 'blunt in colour'. In the Bibliothèque Nationale in Paris is a memorable portrait of Suleiman the

Magnificent in old age, mounted on a horse with three white feet. There is an old Turkish saying which runs:

> One white foot, good-for-nothing horse;
> Two white feet, horse for a beggar;
> Three white feet, horse for a king;
> Four white feet, horse for the knacker.

The painting was made in Istanbul about 1560; though recalling Persian miniatures it has a distinctive Turkish flavour, and the theory that Ottoman miniatures are no more than feeble imitations of Persian has long been abandoned.

17   The Mughals

In the year 1526 the Timurid prince Babur defeated the vast armies of the Afghan Sultan of Delhi, Ibrahim Lodi, on the plain of Panipat and became the first Mughal Emperor of India.[1]

But Islamic architecture, in which the Persian element was usually far stronger than the native, existed of course in India long before the arrival of the Mughals. The Qutb Minar has already been discussed (see page 34), but a splendid example dating from the fourteenth century is to be seen in the mausoleum of Rukn i-Alam at Multan (now in Pakistan). Multan had fallen to Islam as early as the eighth century; it was not, however, until about 1310 that the governor at that time of the Punjab erected the noble mausoleum which was first intended to receive his own ashes. In the event it is those of his spiritual preceptor which lie there.

An octagonal building of buff brick crowned with a white-washed dome, it stands on rising ground and dominates the town. There is some lovely blue and white Timurid-style tilework, much damaged over the years and especially during a siege in 1848 in the Second Sikh War. A curious but very effective feature is the inward-sloping buttressed lowest storey. Within is a mihrab of beautifully carved shisham wood, and the simple sarcophagus of Rukn i-Alam. Such buildings, as Sir Olaf Caroe has pointed out, 'stand to the later Islamic styles rather as do the Romanesque and Norman to the Gothic in our European tradition'.

But to return to Babur. The life story of this remarkable, sensitive and enlightened man, whom we encountered all too briefly when he visited Herat in 1506, may be read in his famous Memoirs — one of the most fascinating and revealing autobiographies ever written, which I discuss in detail in *The Golden Road to Samarkand*, Chapter 10. Like the Florentine renaissance princes he combined a deep love of art and of nature with occasional acts of cruelty which can be understood only if we bear in mind what was universally acceptable in those days; if it is surprising to find a commander-in-chief halting a battle while he counted the number of species of tulips growing wild on the battlefield, it is surely even more surprising to find so civilized a man having his cook flayed alive and his 'taster' hacked to pieces for attempting to poison him. But Babur did both these things.

To Babur we owe the introduction of the Persian-style garden into India, where it was to achieve a greater splendour and variety than ever it did in Iran or Afghanistan. Indeed, Westerners who

[1] The first six Mughal Emperors were: Babur (1526–30), Humayun (1530–40 and 1555–56), Akbar (1556–1605), Jahangir (1605–27), Shah Jahan (1628–58) and Aurangzeb (1658–1707). Their successors are of little interest to us.

visit Shiraz are sometimes disappointed by what this fabled town of roses has to offer; but to those who live in hot or arid countries coolness and greenness, shade and the sound of water gently gliding from ledge to ledge or flowing along marbled runnels, a handful of sweet-scented shrubs and plants and a pavilion or two with a pool and a fountain – these are paradise enough.

Nobody, however, returns from Kashmir unmoved by the magic of the gardens there. More than three hundred years ago the French physician François Bernier, travelling in the train of the Emperor Aurangzeb, spent several months in that 'terrestrial paradise of the Indies' and wrote of the garden at Achibal:

> What principally constitutes the beauty of this place is a fountain, whose waters disperse themselves into a hundred canals round the house . . . and throughout the gardens. . . . The gardens are very handsome, laid out in regular walks, and full of fruit trees – apple, pear, plum, apricot, and cherry. *Jets d'eau* in various forms and fish ponds are in great number, and there is a lofty cascade which in its fall takes the form and colour of a large sheet, thirty or forty paces in length, producing the finest effect imaginable – especially at night, when innumerable lamps, fixed in parts of the wall adapted for that purpose, are lighted under this sheet of water.

Babur had made no fewer than ten gardens in Kabul, his former capital. His favourite was the Garden of Fidelity, of which he once wrote, after visiting it on a golden October day: 'It was at the height of its beauty – its lawns a sheet of clover, the leaves of its pomegranate trees turned to autumnal gold and their fruit a rich red. There were quantities of oranges, but they were not yet ripe; the pomegranates, however, were excellent. . . . I was never so much pleased with the garden of Fidelity as on this occasion.' There is a well-known double-page miniature in the Victoria and Albert Museum showing him instructing his gardeners on the planting of it. From Agra he once sent an urgent order to Kabul for the Belvedere Garden there to be planted 'with the very finest young trees', for lawns to be made and borders to be set with herbs and sweet-smelling flowers. Babur never of course saw his trees mature, and all his gardens have now vanished. The magnificent oriental planes – a tree said to have been introduced in the time of Shah Jehan – are today a striking feature of the Kashmir gardens.

One of the first things that Babur did after making Agra his capital was to find a site for a garden. Lack of water presented a serious problem, but he hoped to solve it by the use of waterwheels. After much searching he discovered a possible spot, had a well sunk and trees planted, a pool made and a house built – 'So, in that charmless and disorderly Hindustan, gardens were laid out in an orderly manner, with borders and parterres everywhere, with roses and narcissi in their proper place.'

OVERLEAF

'Babur making the Garden of Fidelity at Kabul.' Indian miniature, *c.* 1590.

درختهای انار هم هست کردا کرد حوض تمام سه برگزار

بای عن باغ همین است در وقت زرد شدن یابرگهایار بسیار

The Mughals

Of the little that Babur built in Agra in the four or five years that remained to him, even less has survived. The reign of his beloved but unworthy son, Humayun, was interrupted by the invasion in 1540 of an Afghan, Sher Shah – sometimes wrongly described as a usurper – who obliged the Emperor to seek refuge in Persia and Afghanistan. To Sher Shah we owe the splendid mausoleum which he ordered to be erected at Sahsaram, in Bengal, in which Islamic and native Indian styles are happily wedded. The building, which is of red sandstone, rises magnificently from a granite platform cornered with little domed pavilions (*chatris*), while the whole complex seems to float on the surface of an artificial lake (*hauz*) which duplicates its beauty by reflection. The flattened dome, round whose great supporting octagon cluster further pavilions, rises to a height of more than one hundred and fifty feet above the water. Sahsaram means 'a thousand toys', the town deriving its name from a legendary once-resident demon whose thousand arms each held a separate plaything.

Sher Shah also built the magnificent Old Fort in Delhi, with its splendid mosque within the walls. Of this, Sir Olaf Caroe wrote in *The Pathans*:

> The mighty gates and battlements of his old citadel at Delhi give the measure of the man; those formidable bastions make the Red Fort of Shah Jahan, three miles away to the north, look like the puny castellations of a child, neatly put together from a box of bricks. Sher Shah's mosque within his citadel has a simple, noble grace all its own, more in harmony surely with the true inspirations of Islam than any of those pearly caskets built by the Mughals to the glory of God.

Humayun is remembered chiefly as the father of the great Akbar, in whose reign an impressive mausoleum was erected at Delhi by Humayun's widow to contain the mortal remains of her husband, who died from falling downstairs; native builders in the Middle East still fail to appreciate the dangers that result from steps whose rises and treads are not constant. The building was designed by a Muslim architect, perhaps from Samarkand, and but for some Hindu-style cupolas is pure Iranian; it is generally considered to be the prototype of the far more lovely and more famous Taj Mahal. The octagonal domed tomb chamber and the four octagonal towers that support it stand on an enormous podium, twenty-two feet in height, with arches ornamented with white marble; it was finished about 1570. The formal gardens, though now bleak, are of interest for being the oldest in India that preserve the original layout. It was at the mausoleum of Humayun that, in 1857, Hodson ('Hodson of Hodson's Horse') received the surrender of Bahadur Shah, last of the Mughal emperors.

Twenty-three miles from Agra is the famous ghost city of Fatehpur Sikri; 'Fatehpur' means 'Victory City'. A certain

Shaikh Salim Chishti, a hermit living in this arid and rocky
district, had prophesied that Akbar, who had no son and heir,
would become the father of three male infants; when, therefore,
his Rajput wife became pregnant he sent her to bear the child
(the future Jahangir) in the village of Sikri. On the birth of a
second son – and a third was to follow in due course – he was so
persuaded of the piety of the Shaikh and the sanctity of the place
that he decided to create a new capital there.

Building after building – a mosque, palaces, audience
chambers, baths, stables, a circus for polo and elephant combats,
houses for his courtiers, and so on – rose in swiftest succession
and a chequered courtyard was designed so that Akbar could play
human chess with dancing-girls for pieces. Gardens were planted
with cypresses and jasmine, blue-and-white dovecotes installed,
a large lake constructed, and the whole palace complex surrounded by walls of red sandstone; and such was the speed with which

this royal city sprang up that Ralph Fitch, one of the first English-men to visit India,[1] who came to Agra and Fatehpur Sikri in 1584 or 1585, could describe them as 'two very great cities, either of them much greater than London and very populous'.

Then a few months after Fitch's visit, something happened – probably the failure of the water supply – to make Akbar cut his losses, abandon his dream city to the jackals and bring back his court to Agra. Today Fatehpur Sikri is empty; deserted, but not devastated; the most beautiful, the best-tended museum in all India:

> 'Bats hang under the domes, wild bees fly in and out. Palaces of the Emperor's wives and favourites are carved like jewel boxes. Only one of the desolate courtyards holds any sign of the present – the courtyard of the tomb of the pro-phesying hermit Salim Chishti. Barren women come and tie strips of cloth to the fretted screens of the tomb, hoping that their wombs will be opened.'[2]

The Boland Darwaza (or 'Lofty Gateway') of the great mosque was built by Akbar to commemorate his victories. Another Englishman, William Finch, who came to Fatehpur Sikri in 1610 to find its buildings 'lying waste without inhabitants', considered this gateway 'one of the highest and fairest (I suppose) in the whole world; on the top are a number of clustering pinnacles, curiously disposed'; they have been less poetically described as 'a row of piss-pots inverted'. High up on the Boland Darwaza may be read this curious inscription: 'Isa [Jesus], on whom be peace, said: "The world is a bridge: pass over it, but build no house on it. The world endures but an hour; spend it in devotion."' Salim Chishti's tomb, in white marble, is perfect in detail and repair, as is also the House of Worship with its remarkable central pillar.

Akbar, while building at Agra, also found time to beautify and fortify Lahore (Pakistan), which was to be further embellished by his successors. His handsome tomb at Sikandra, just outside Agra – one of the most original of Mughal monuments – was com-pleted by his son Jahangir in 1613. Jahangir, who was a great lover of gardens, was also responsible for a charming Pearl Mosque at Lahore, his principal place of residence.

The reign of Shah Jahan (1628–58) witnessed the golden age of Mughal architecture, and among the many noble buildings erected by order of the Emperor none is more justly famous or more peerless than the Taj Mahal at Agra, built as a mausoleum to contain the body of his favourite wife, Mumtaz-i-Mahal ('the Elect of the Palace'), who died in 1629 when giving birth to her fourteenth child. It is said – on slender evidence – that the architect was a certain Ustad Isa, a Persian from Shiraz, and with more probability that craftsmen from all over Asia, and even a

OPPOSITE

'Slaughter in a Mughal camp.' A particularly graphic miniature from an *Akbar-nama*, late sixteenth century.

[1] The first Englishman known to have set foot on Indian soil was Father Stevens, a Jesuit, in 1579.

[2] *Places*, ed. by Geoffrey Grigson and others, Grosvenor Press, London, 1954.

The Mughals

OPPOSITE

Delhi. The Pearl
Mosque in the Red
Fort, 1659. Built by
Aurangzeb of white
and pearl-grey
marble.

OVERLEAF RIGHT

Agra. The Taj Mahal,
c. 1635. Shah Jahan's
immortal tribute to
his favourite wife,
Mumtaz-i-Mahal
('The Elect of the
Palace'), who died in
childbirth in 1629.

OVERLEAF LEFT

'The Emperor Babur
receiving Uzbeg and
Rajput envoys in a
garden at Agra on
18th December,
1528.' Painted by
Ram Das in 1590.

master goldsmith from distant France, were summoned by Shah Jahan to enhance the beauty of this indestructible tribute to his beloved Mumtaz. It is the most Persian of the great Indian imperial mausoleums, yet there is nothing quite like it in all Iran.

'Looking at the Taj by moonlight' has become a music-hall joke; but those who come to Agra to scoff remain to marvel. As Lord Roberts wrote after his first sight of the Taj in 1857: 'Neither words nor pencil could give to the most imaginative reader the slightest idea of the all-satisfying beauty and purity of this glorious conception. To those who have not already seen it, I would say: "Go to India. The Taj alone is worth the journey. . . ."' The dazzling white marble (with coloured inlay) is as perfect now as on the day it left the hand of the stonemason; yet who could wish that Time, which softens the asperities of Gothic cathedrals, had laid a mellowing hand on the Taj? Like the tilework on a Persian mosque or the white and glittering gold interior of a Bavarian rococo church, this marble demands to be seen in all its pristine purity.

The white marble interior of the mausoleum is exquisitely ornamented with inlay of coloured marbles of the kind known as *pietra dura*. In the centre of the building is the cenotaph of Mumtaz-i-Mahal and, beside her, that of her husband, who had originally intended to build, on the further bank of the Jumna, a second mausoleum in *black* marble to receive his own ashes. Aurangzeb, Shah Jahan's third son and successor who in 1658 deposed his father and imprisoned him in the Red Fort at Agra, enclosed the two tombs with a magnificent screen of pierced marble once inlaid with precious stones – an act, perhaps, of contribution for his unfilial behaviour. And then – to flatter by imitation? – he built for his own wife a miniature and pinched version of the Taj at Aurangabad in the Deccan.

It should be borne in mind that what we tend to think of as the Taj Mahal is, in fact, only a single (though the principal) building of a whole complex – the subsidiary buildings, in which a good deal of use has been made of red sandstone, serving admirably as a foil to the mausoleum. The perfection of the ensemble is perhaps best appreciated when we view it – the energetic at dawn, the slugabeds at sunset – from the far bank of the Jumna. To Shah Jahan we also owe, among much else, the many sumptuous buildings in the forts at Agra and Delhi. The Pearl Mosque in the former was proclaimed by Fergusson 'one of the purest and most elegant buildings of its class to be found anywhere. . . . The moment you enter by the Eastern gateway the effect of its court-yard is surpassingly beautiful.' That in Delhi is hardly less attractive.

The splendid aquatints of Indian buildings made by the two Daniells, Thomas and his nephew William, and published in their *Oriental Scenery* (1795–1808), created a short-lived vogue in England for '"Gothick" paraphrases of Muslim architecture'

which culminated in Humphrey Repton and John Nash's designs for the Brighton Pavilion;[1] thus Sydney Smith, in his famous quip that St Paul's went to Brighton 'and pupped', was maligning that blameless cathedral.

In the reign of Aurangzeb began the steady decline of Muslim architecture in India. With the opening of the nineteenth century came handsome British neo-Classical buildings in brick coated with plaster, reminiscent of the Regency style in London and elsewhere. Of Government House at Calcutta (completed in 1803) it might reasonably be maintained that Kedleston Hall had gone to India 'and pupped', thus provoking Lord Curzon's no less famous protest that Government House was 'only of lăth and plăster; *my* house is of ălăbăster'. There followed in due course 'the mingled Gothic-Saracenic fantasies of the Victorians'. Finally was heard the sound of what Olaf Caroe has called 'the magnificent organ note of Lutyens and Baker at New Delhi'. But that has nothing to do with Islam.

Though Babur is said to have brought many fine Timurid manuscripts with him to India, it seems probable that Humayun's enforced exile, and especially that part of it which he spent at Shah Tahmasp's guest at Tabriz, was chiefly responsible for the foundation of the Mughal school of painting. Two Tabrizi artists, Mir Sayyid Ali and Abd al-Samad, certainly followed him from Tabriz to Kabul and presumably joined him in India after his return there in 1555. Abd al-Samad, incidentally, is said to have written the whole of the very short 112th chapter of the Koran on a single poppy seed.

It is possible that a very large and most unusual court scene, painted on cotton and showing Timurid princes in a garden pavilion, was the work of Mir Sayyid Ali and Abd al-Samad. It is completely Persian in composition and in treatment; but soon the Indian miniaturists were to develop a highly individual style which makes their paintings immediately recognizable.

Mughal artists were exceptional in that they illustrated actual historical incidents – as, for example, Akbar inspecting the progress of his building operations at Fatehpur Sikri. They also approached portraiture in much the same spirit as did European draughtsmen such as Holbein and François Clouet, something not common in Iran even under the Safavids. It was in the reign of Akbar – a great patron of the art of the book although he himself could neither read nor write – that Mughal painting reached its zenith. Father Antonio Monserrate, a Jesuit at Akbar's court from 1579 to 1582, wrote:

> He has built a workshop near the palace, where also are studios for the finer and more reputable arts, such as painting, goldsmith work, tapestry making, carpet and curtain making, and the manufacture of arms. Hither he very frequently comes

[1] See Mildred Archer, *Indian Architecture and the British*, Country Life Books, 1968, in which may be read a fuller account of Sezincote and the Brighton Pavilion.

and relaxes his mind with watching at their work those who practise these arts.[1]

Akbar's religious unorthodoxy allowed him to encourage the representation of human beings and animals, a liberty constantly taken by court artists in Islamic countries though never, of course in a Koran. He once said:

> It appears to me as if a painter had quite peculiar means of recognizing God, for a painter in sketching anything that has life, and in devising the limbs one after another, must come to feel that he cannot bestow personality on his work, and is thus forced to thank God, the giver of life, and thus increase his knowledge.

Jahangir, though an opium-eater and a drunkard, was steadied by a very remarkable wife and so survived to rule for twenty-two years. A generous patron of artists, he wrote in his Memoirs: 'I am very fond of pictures, and have such discrimination in judging them that I can tell the name of the artist, whether living or dead;' and he added that if several artists had worked on a picture he could 'declare without fail by whom the brow and by whom the eyelashes were drawn.'[2] His deep love of animals was exemplified by his employment of artists to record unusual species, though hardly (one must feel) by his personal game-bag of 17,167 birds and mammals. The splendour continued under Shah Jahan, but we remember him more for his Taj Mahal and other buildings than as a patron of the art of the book. Then the decline set in, with European and native influences increasingly in evidence.

England, as might be expected, has exceptionally fine collections of Indian manuscripts;[3] but probably the grandest of all, the enormous *Hamsa-nama* made for Akbar (with pages 27 inches by 21 inches) is in the Metropolitan Museum in New York, and in most great libraries throughout the world Mughal painting is well represented.

OPPOSITE

Kabul, Afghanistan. Babur's grave, above which Jahangir erected the headstone in the early seventeenth century.

[1] This and the two following quotations are taken from Laurence Binyon's *The Court Painters of the Grand Moguls*, Oxford University Press, 1921.

[2] Dr Bode, the eminent German art historian, made his attributions by a study of the artist's manner of treating ears, fingers and toes.

[3] Principally in the British Museum, the India Office Library, the Victoria and Albert Museum, and the Bodleian at Oxford.

Postscript

Thus we come to the end of this brief survey of the architecture, painting and 'minor' arts of the Islamic world. Little has been said about what has been achieved in the last two hundred years, and nothing about the remoter outposts of Islam, which is the dominant religion in about one third of all Africa, including Somalia; in a part of the Malagasy Republic (Madagascar), and in much of Indonesia. As a world religion it is numerically second in importance only to Christianity, with a total adherance of little less than four hundred millions, about nine-tenths of whom are Sunnis. Impressive modern mosques have been built in such far-flung places as Penang and Kuala Lumpur (Malaysia), Brunei (Borneo), Jakarta (Java) and Ibadan (Nigeria), while all over the world Muslims have erected places of worship in countries where they are in a small minority. Even Leningrad has a handsome mosque whose dome appears to be a close imitation of that of the Gur-i-Mir in Samarkand. These buildings generally follow traditional patterns, but there are a few which demonstrate that Islam is on occasion ready to move – architecturally, at all events – with the times.

Small Persian ceramic bottle in the shape of a cat, sixteenth or seventeenth century.

The Centres of Historic Islam

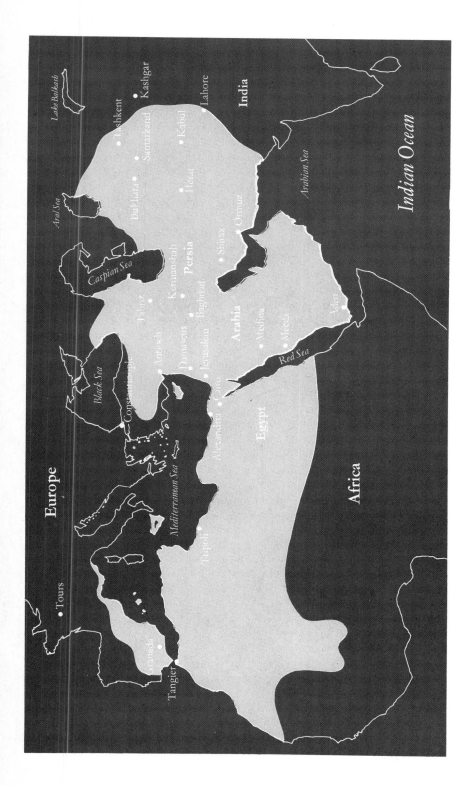

Lake Balkash
Kashgar
Ashkent
Lahore
India
Samarkand
Kabul
Bukhara
Herat
Aral Sea
Arabian Sea
Indian Ocean
Shiraz
Ormuz
Caspian Sea
Kermanshah
Persia
Tabriz
Baghdad
Arabia
Aden
Antioch
Damascus
Medina
Mecca
Black Sea
Jerusalem
Constantinople
Red Sea
Cairo
Alexandria
Egypt
Mediterranean Sea
Africa
Europe
Tripoli
Tours
Granada
Tangier

For Further Reading

Archer, Mildred. *Indian Architecture and the British*. Country Life Books, 1968.

Binyon, Laurence. *Court Painters of the Great Moghuls*. Oxford University Press, 1921.

Binyon, Laurence, editor. *Khamsa* of Nizami, 1539–43. The Studio, 1928.

Blunt, Wilfrid. *The Golden Road to Samarkand*. Hamish Hamilton, 1973.

Blunt, Wilfrid. *Isfahan, Pearl of Persia*. Elek, 1974.

Blunt, Wilfrid. *A Persian Spring*. Barrie, 1957.

Caroe, Sir Olaf. *The Pathans*. London, 1957.

Chelebi, Evliya. *Narrative of Travels* . . . . Oriental Translation Fund, 1834, 1846.

Dozy, Reinhart. *Spanish Islam*. London, 1913.

Edwards, A. C. *The Legacy of Persia*. Edited by A. J. Arberry. Oxford University Press, 1953.

Erdmann, Kurt. *Seven Hundred Years of Oriental Carpets*. Faber, 1970.

Fedden, Robin. *Syria*. Robert Hale, 1946.

Fergusson, James. *History of Indian and Eastern Architecture*. London, 1876.

Ford, Richard. *A Handbook for Travellers in Spain*. John Murray, 1845.

Glück, Heinrich, and Diez, Ernst. *Die Kunst des Islam*. Berlin, 1925.

Grube, Ernst. *The World of Islam*. Hamlyn, 1966.

Handbook for Travellers in Asia Minor. John Murray, 1895.

Hill, Derek, and Grabar, Otto. *Islamic Architecture and its Decoration*. Faber, 1964.

Horne, John. *Many Days in Morocco*. London.

McCabe, Joseph. *The Splendours of Moorish Spain*. London, 1935.

Pope, Arthur Upham, and Ackerman, Phyllis, editors. *A Survey of Persian Art*. Oxford University Press, 1939.

Stevens, Sir Roger. *Land of The Great Sophy*. Methuen, 1962.

Notes on the Illustrations

Abbreviations used in the notes are:

59	RHA: Richard Ashworth.
60	RHA: Sybil Sassoon.
63	RHA: Tony Hutt.
64	RHA: Tony Hutt.
65	RHA: Tony Hutt.
66	MEA: Alistair Duncan.
68	Bluett & Sons, London. Photo: CBL.
70	By courtesy of the author.
71	Photo: Josephine Powell.
73	RHA: Sybil Sassoon.
74–5	RHA: Richard Ashworth.
75	RHA: Robert Harding.
76–7	RHA: Richard Ashworth.
77	RHA: Tony Hutt.
78–9	RHA: Robert Harding.
80	RHA: Robert Harding.
83	RHA: Sybil Sassoon.
84	Photo: Josephine Powell.
87	RHA: Robert Harding.
89	British Museum. Photo: Michael Holford.
91	Royal Asiatic Society, London. Photo: British Museum.
93	By courtesy of the author.
94	British Museum.
95	Royal Asiatic Society. Photo: British Museum.
99	RHA: Robert Harding.
100	RHA: Richard Ashworth.
102	By courtesy of the author.
104	V & A. Photo: CBL.
106	Tehran Museum. RHA: Richard Ashworth.
107	RHA: Robert Ellis.
108	V & A. Photo: CBL.
108–9	British Museum.
110	V & A. Photo: CBL.
112	Christie, Manson and Woods. Photo: Rainbird.
113	Private collection. Photo: Rainbird.
115	Christie, Manson and Woods. Photo: Rainbird.
116	V & A. Photo: Rainbird.
118	Österreichisches Museum für angewandte Kunst, Vienna.
120	RHA: J. E. Edwards.
122	By courtesy of the author.
123	Shiraz Museum. RHA: Robert Harding.
124	RHA: Christina Gascoigne.
126	By courtesy of the author.
130–31	V & A. Photos: Rainbird.
133	V & A. RHA: Christina Gascoigne.
134	V & A. RHA: Christina Gascoigne.
137	RHA: Christina Gascoigne.
138–9	RHA: Christina Gascoigne.
139	V & A. Photo: CBL.
140 top	RHA: Tony Hutt.
140 bottom	RHA: Bill and Clare Leimbach.
142	RHA: Christina Gascoigne.
144	Photo: Josephine Powell.
146	V & A. Photo: CBL.
147	Cartography: Tom Stalker-Miller. Artwork: Rainbird.

Index

Page numbers in *italic* type indicate illustrations.

Index